ROBERT VICKREY
Master of Magic Realism
A RETROSPECTIVE EXHIBITION

ROBERT VICKREY
Master of Magic Realism
A RETROSPECTIVE EXHIBITION

H. Alexander Rich
Editor & Gallery Director

J. William Meek, III
Guest Curator

Jenna Rice
Gallery Curator

Melvin Art Gallery • Florida Southern College
Lakeland, Florida
SEPTEMBER 4 - NOVEMBER 4, 2015

Catalogue of the exhibition "Robert Vickrey: Master of Magic Realism," organized by
J. William Meek, III and the Melvin Art Gallery of Florida Southern College.
ISBN 978-0-578-16900-2

Catalogue Design by H. Alexander Rich

Cover: Detail from *Street Surfer* (1986) by Robert Vickrey,
in the Collection of William and Barbara Meek

CONTENTS

FOREWORD

Florida Southern College is honored to host a retrospective exhibition on the art of Robert Vickrey, who would have turned ninety years old in August 2016. A master of the egg-tempera medium and a so-called Magic Realist painter, Vickrey (1926 - 2011) is a testament to artistic resilience, consistent in his manner and intent, even when his chosen style fell in and out of favor with the art-world establishment. Over the course of his six-decade career, Vickrey remained unapologetic about his technique: "I PAINT ALL MY PICTURES IN MY HEAD. Most of them are dreamscapes more than anything else."

Vickrey was born in Manhattan during the dog days of summer in August 1926. Eighty-four years later in April 2011, he passed away at his home in Naples, Florida. In the spectacularly prolific and successful years in between, the Yale-trained painter made a name for himself in the art world as a conjurer of hyper-realist scenes whose tinges of the fantastic or the slightly odd elevated them to a sphere beyond mere Realism.

At the height of a frenzy in the American art world for scenes depicting a mix of the ostensibly "real" and the quizzically fantastic, Vickrey's "Magic Realist" paintings received great public notice in the 1950s and 1960s. He went on to become a go-to portrait artist for *TIME* magazine, was the subject of a PBS documentary, and saw more than a thousand pieces of his work enter nationwide collections both public — from the Metropolitan Museum of Art and the Whitney in New York to the Corcoran and Smithsonian Museums in D.C. — and private, like that of William and Barbara Hanson Meek, Florida Southern alumni ('72 and '76, respectively) whose beneficence has enabled this retrospective.

Even when many in the art world turned away from all types of Realism in favor of abstract or conceptual art, Vickrey stuck to his stylistic guns; while never replicating or fixating on a single subject or tone for his work (some are more psychologically tense, whereas others seem more playful and child-like), he always held true to a style that is undoubtedly and inimitably his own. Although his art was regarded for a time as too illustrative (a criticism other artists like Andrew Wyeth and Norman Rockwell suffered), Vickrey found a new surge of attention beginning in the 1980s, as interest in Magic Realism came back to the fore.

As this exhibition makes clear, Vickrey's work features many recurrent motifs that allow viewers to assess certain preoccupations and major themes of his career, from his use of shadows and bicycles to the solitary Saint Vincent nuns and children surrounded by mysteriously floating balloons. The great through-line of Vickrey's paintings, though, is that there is always something slightly uncanny — just a bit off about these painted worlds — where the situations depicted within seem real and unreal, relatable and yet eerily strange at the same time (see p. 13).

Just as when we awaken from our most realistic dreams, having only moments before believed the actuality of everything we have just witnessed, Vickrey's paintings draw us in and push us to seek out clear narratives where no narratives may be.

We can never figure out exactly what Vickrey hopes to symbolize with any given canvas. Each painting will evoke something distinct in each viewer — be it puzzlement, delight, angst, or nostalgia — but that is just as this master of Magic Realism intended it. Throughout a remarkable career in and out of the spotlight, Vickrey gave us his uncanny dreamscapes as starting points upon which our individual thoughts can run free.

H. Alexander Rich, Ph.D.
Director, Melvin & Burks Galleries
Assistant Professor of Art History
Florida Southern College

Robert Vickrey, A Tribute

This special Memorial exhibition for the American master Robert Vickrey (1926-2011) is the second time the Melvin and Burks Galleries at FSC has hosted a Vickrey exhibition, the first occurring in 1988. It is also the artist's second memorial exhibition; the first was hosted a year ago by the Fort Wayne Museum of Art in Indiana, a show I also curated.

In 1988, Professor Downing Barnitz asked his former student to curate an exhibition of Vickrey's important egg tempera creations. This current exhibition was requested by Dr. Jim Rogers and enthusiastically supported by Dr. Alex Rich.

Vickrey's association with FSC actually began quite innocently when the artist submitted a painting for a purchase prize competition at Southern in 1952. The $200 prize meant much to the young artist who had graduated just a few years earlier from the Yale School of Fine Arts. Whereabouts of this painting once exhibited at the college have remained a mystery for decades. The year before a major work had been selected for the Whitney Museum of American Art "Annual Exhibition" and subsequently purchased by the museum for its permanent collection. Since that time another ninety museums have acquired his paintings including the Metropolitan Museum of Art. In 1952 Vickrey was still with his first gallery representative in New York City but by the next year would be coaxed away by the prominent Midtown Galleries, which would represent him for the next twenty-five years.

After graduating from Southern in the spring of 1972 I joined the Harmon Gallery as assistant director that fall. I took my first trip with gallery founder Foster Harmon to New York City almost immediately and visited the Midtown Galleries with him to select Vickrey paintings from their stock to exhibit at the gallery in Naples. Vickrey would not learn of our gallery's interest in his work until 1981.

In 1981, after having acquired the gallery from Harmon in 1978 with my wife Barbara Hanson Meek (FSC '76), I was able to persuade Vickrey to be represented directly, and

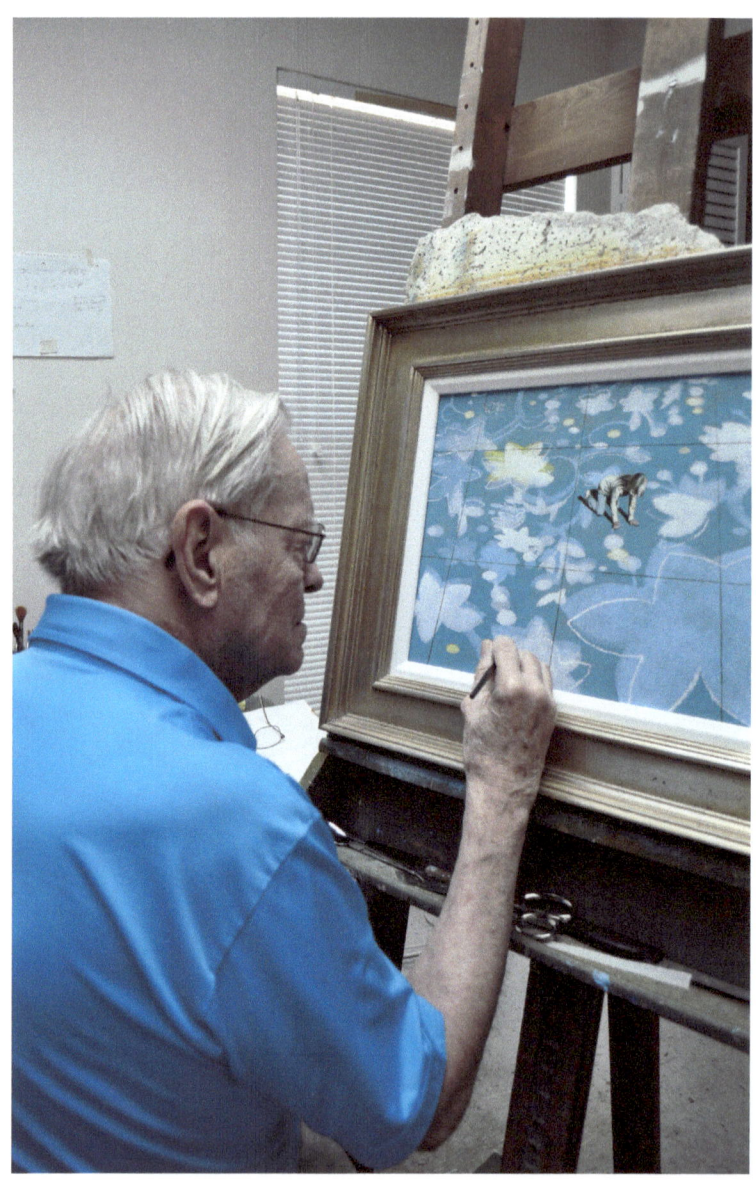

Robert Vickrey at work in 2010

we hosted our first solo exhibition of his work in the spring of 1982. Within five years we were outselling his New York City gallery, and our relationship with the artist grew into a strong friendship — and now primary representative of his small estate of paintings. (Fewer than eighty paintings are in his estate compared to the Andy Warhol estate, which has about ninety-four thousand works).

Vickrey has other interesting attributes such as always being represented by a major New York City gallery for fifty continuous years (1951 - 2001). He had nearly one hundred solo exhibitions during his life, two thirds of which were at art museums. (His last exhibition was one I curated for the Boca Raton Museum of Art, which opened just a week after his death in 2011). John Canaday, art critic for the *New York Times* wrote in the 1970s that Vickrey was the most proficient American artist using the egg tempera medium. Two noted art historians have written books about the artist: in 2005, Donald Miller, former art critic for the *Pittsburgh Post-Gazette*, wrote a book about Vickrey's use of the Saint Vincent nuns as subjects in his paintings for over fifty years, and, in 2009, art historian Dr. Philip Eliasoph of Fairfield University in Connecticut wrote a large monograph about the artist published by Hudson Hills Press. For ten years starting in 1958, Vickrey created eighty paintings of famous people for the covers of *TIME*, more than half of which are now in the National Portrait Gallery.

All of this was done during a period in American and world art when abstract art was king and every ten years produced a new "ism" in art. To remain true to what he felt was important in art and not be swayed by current popular trends in the art world should ensure that Vickrey will remain a historical figure in American art history forever.

J. William Meek, III
Guest Curator
Director Emeritus
Harmon-Meek Gallery

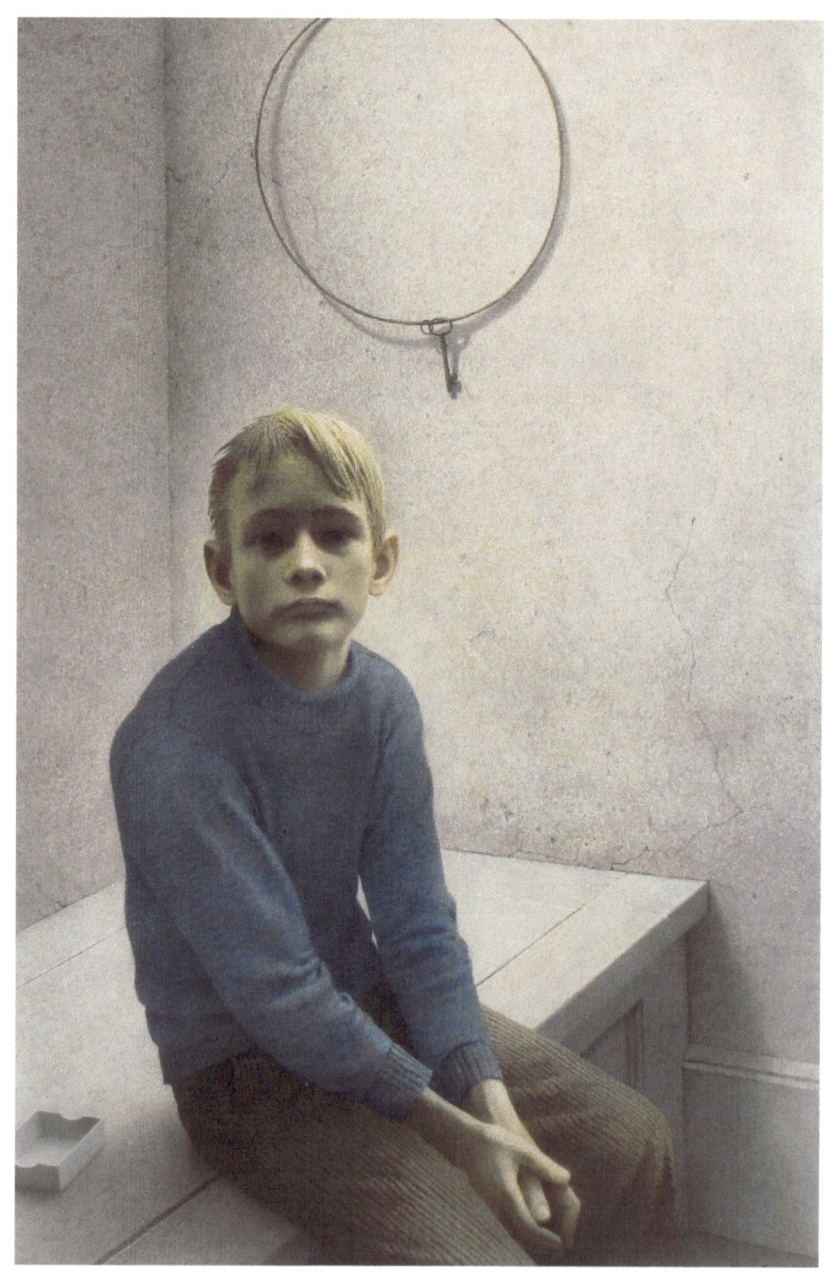

The Corner Seat, 1971

Melvin Art Gallery | ROBERT VICKREY: *Master of Magic Realism*

The Uncanny Appeal of Robert Vickrey's Magic Realism

Robert Vickrey (August 26, 1926 – April 17, 2011) may not be a household name when it comes to twentieth-century American artists, but the trajectory and reception of his work over the course of a six-decade career bespeak the changing predilections and fickleness of the art world.

There can be little doubt that Vickrey was a master of his craft. Not only is his work painted magisterially with regard to its naturalism and his handling of his signature egg-tempera medium, but part of the great appeal of Vickrey's paintings is also how deftly they balance elusiveness and accessibility. There is a sense of the uncanny intertwined with a timelessness that makes Vickrey's works — in this show ranging from 1958 to 2011 — startlingly relatable and contemporary-looking, even from the perspective of 2015.

One might expect to be put off by the enigmatic aura of much of Vickrey's painted subject matter; his work certainly reads as peculiar at times — not because it is overtly peculiar, but because the source of the peculiar feeling evoked by it is difficult to locate. Usually there is nothing inherently "wrong" in terms of the reality conveyed in the paintings. Everything looks right. Everything looks real. But something seems odd.

Among Vickrey's many repeated motifs, it may be the long shadows or the bird's-eye perspective in a work like *Red, Yellow & Green* (1995, p. 42) or the balloons that seem to float around, sometimes perceptibly as in *Moonlit Patterns* (2010, p. 64) and at other times seemingly unseen by the figures in works like *Monet's Gossips* (1995, page 43), that give these paintings a sense of the extra-ordinary. Yet rather than alienating, the mystery laced into many of Vickrey's paintings becomes alternatively alluring to the viewer, who seeks edifying narratives or explanations within them.

Indeed, when we look at a painting like *The Corner Seat* (1971, opposite), with a boy seated in a corner with shoulders turned in and a sullen expression on his face, we want for a narrative explanation (the lay viewer cannot know this is a portrait of Vickrey's son). The feeling evoked by the painting is reminiscent of childhood angst or punishment, but the setting is unnerving in its starkness, its lighting, and its sparing use of what we are pushed cleverly by Vickrey to presume are the symbolic props that may reveal the story to us. We are not privy to that story, though, but are drawn in by the familiarity of the situation amidst the uncanny "just-not-right-ness" projected by the scene. We know deep down that something curious is going on, although usually, as in this case, we cannot isolate what that curiosity is.

As early as his first exhibition notice appearing in the *New York Times* in February 1951, critics were already trying to pinpoint the feelings evoked by and the manner employed in Vickrey's work, but — even at so early a moment in his career — struggled to do so.

Robert Vickrey, making a debut at the Creative Gallery, lets a meticulous technique and a realistic style serve a fantastic imagination. Full of obliquely expressed sympathy for the human situation, his canvases are "problem pictures." In vivid and original ways, they symbolize loneliness or hostility or simply the pains of growing up. Those who like "subjects" will be delighted by this new talent.[1]

Although calling his paintings "problem pictures" seems quaint today, the *Times* reviewer first encountering Vickrey's work already ascribes to it its signature mix of reality and fantasy and nods at the indiscernibility created by that problematic amlagam, pondering exactly what these canvases seem to symbolize. Is it loneliness the critic detects? Or is that hostility? Is it both? Or maybe it seems so eerily familiar because it conjures childhood angst?

Eight months later, in December 1951, Vickrey's work is described differently and — remarkably — in the same terms used to describe him sixty-four years later in our 2015 exhibition. A brief *Times* capsule summary of current New York City shows assigns a new designation to Vickrey: "This young magic realist thinks up disturbing and poetic subject-matter."[2] The term "Magic Realism" and its application to art was still fairly new at that time. It gained widespread notice in the art world in 1943 via a Museum of Modern Art exhibition entitled "Americans 1943: Realists and Magic Realists."

Defined by Alfred H. Barr as "a term sometimes applied to the work of painters who by means of an exact realistic technique try to make plausible and convincing their improbable, dreamlike or fantastic visions,"[3] Magic Realism entered the popular lexicon in the United States as an art term mainly to apply to American art, in particular, in order to distinguish it from its ostensible European antecedent Surrealism (although work by Picasso, Miró, and Magritte had been described as "Magic Realist" in the previous decade). For many collectors, museums, and galleries, Magic Realism became an exciting and favored alternative to the Realism that had long been acquainted with Pre-World War II American art.

Yet, despite dubbing Vickrey a trendy Magic Realist, two days later the *New York Times* drops the Magic Realist reference, re-defining Vickrey yet again, now as a "Symbolist," appraising:

Robert Vickrey . . . is a symbolic realist. His scenes are probably not those of common experience and yet they furnish acceptable correspondences with general feelings of disquiet. His fine, steely paint surfaces owe something to Andrew Wyeth, but his art is far less local in significance. There is a menace in the shadow cast across a closed door . . .[4]

This third *Times* summary touches upon something essential in Vickrey's work and the ironic effect of its uncanniness on viewers: it may be in its not mimicking anyone's "common experience" that it becomes all the more open to engaging countless people with memories of their own lives and their own "general feelings of disquiet." Vickrey's success as a painter lies in his incontrovertible engagement with the viewer, both with regard to the perceived familiarity evoked by his paintings and by necessitating that the viewer search for answers likely undiscoverable within them. If one tries to find the exact source of the uncanny in Vickrey's paintings, he or she will typically fail; but rather than be frustrated by not finding answers — after all, part of the fun of the uncanny is understanding that the uncanny cannot be made canny at all — the viewer remains engrossed by the knowingness that something, just something, is not right here.

Thus, the term "problem" painter. Or Magic Realist. Or Symbolic Realist. Obviously, placing Vickrey as an artist is not a simple task. Each early review tries to illustrate in words that which is readily recognized visually in Vickrey's pictures. We all know something uncanny when we see it. It may be difficult to figure out what it is exactly that makes that which we see as uncanny uncanny, but we know it is uncanny nonetheless. This is the experience of looking at a Vickrey painting. There is something uncanny about it, and, because we all know and share in our comprehension of its uncanniness, it becomes relatable to all.

Magic Realism entails this innate human sense of the uncanny, the feeling that you know something is not quite right but also know that you cannot quite put your finger on that which is not quite right. As a result, the term that has stuck most persistently to Vickrey, then, is Magic Realist. And he is undoubtedly a Magic Realist. But what his brand of Magic Realism is — precisely — is harder to define. All Magic Realism, by virtue of its being simultaneously "magical" and "realist," is an uncertainty. It is real and yet not real. Familiar yet alien. Dream-like yet grounded in what appears to be the real world. Magic Realism grapples with the idea that the fantastic or the magical or the surreal can exist simultaneously with the real. Vickrey's work *is* certainly Magic Realist, but searching for the oddity that makes it so can be a thrillingly evasive puzzle for any viewer.

Sometimes feelings or memories are hard to put into words or seem almost too fantastical to describe to others; this is almost what we see in Vickrey's works. Scenes like *Caroline's Sailor Suit* (1987, p. 32) or *A Difficult Lie* (2006, p. 53) are steeped in eerie and at times discomfiting psychological tension, "real" but for their unique oddities. Just like the idiosyncrasies and quirks of everyday existence each of us encounters in our own individual lives, no one can feel the same way about or explicate one's sense of self or place perfectly. And these paintings seem to tap into that complexity of human psychology and the dream state, the difficulty in conveying that which is beyond the merely visual aspect of lived experience.

Unlike, say, a Dalí painting that takes place in a hyper-realistically painted alternative "Dalí" landscape — often deserts set impossibly by seas and populated by biomorphic creatures — Vickrey's paintings offer deceptively realistic dreamscapes that exist plainly in an earthly realm. The subject matter within the scenes could easily play out in the real world and could easily be re-created; the underlying incongruities within them, however, and the lack of explanation for the narratives underlying the subject matter leave the viewer puzzled and intensely aware of the uncanny within.

This is the gift of Vickrey's Magic Realism, and that is why the very experience of looking at Vickrey's work is Magic Realist in itself. As viewers, we feel at once drawn to his work but at the same time estranged from and slightly put off from it. The odd congruities between comfort and discomfort are what make Vickrey's work so inherently intriguing and, at their core, what makes them so timeless.

H. Alexander Rich, Ph.D.
Director, Melvin & Burks Galleries
Assistant Professor of Art History
Florida Southern College

Notes

1. "Vedova Paintings on Exhibition Here: His Works Are On Display at Viviano Gallery—5 Other Shows Also Viewed," *New York Times* (February 10, 1951): L11.

2. "In Brief: Exhibitions," *New York Times* (December 14, 1951): X11.

3. "Americans 1943: Realists and Magic Realists" Museum of Modern Art press release, February 2, 1943.

4. Stuart Preston, "Among Recent Openings," *New York Times* (December 16, 1951): X11.

Opposite:
Manikin, 1975 (detail)

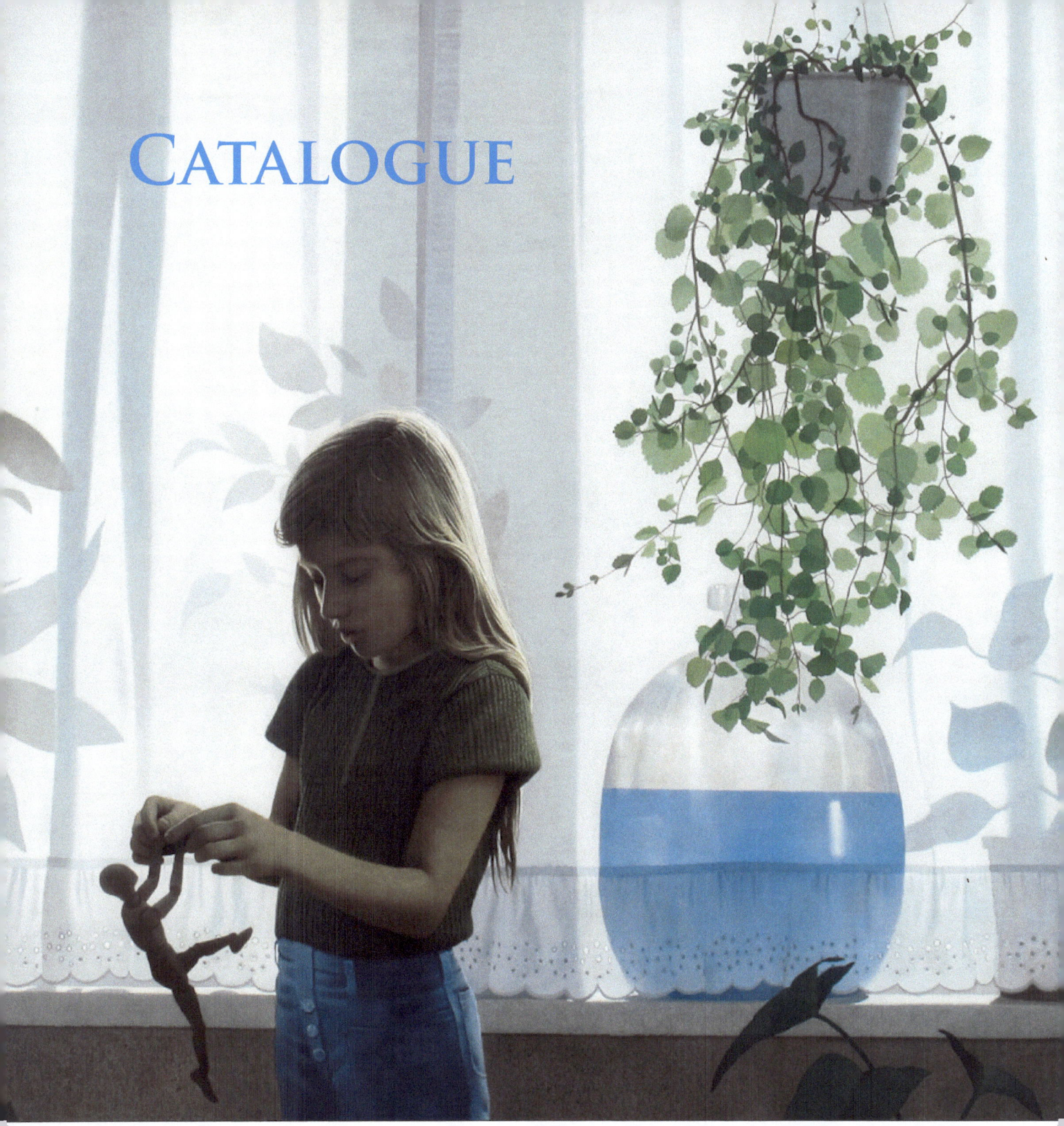

CATALOGUE

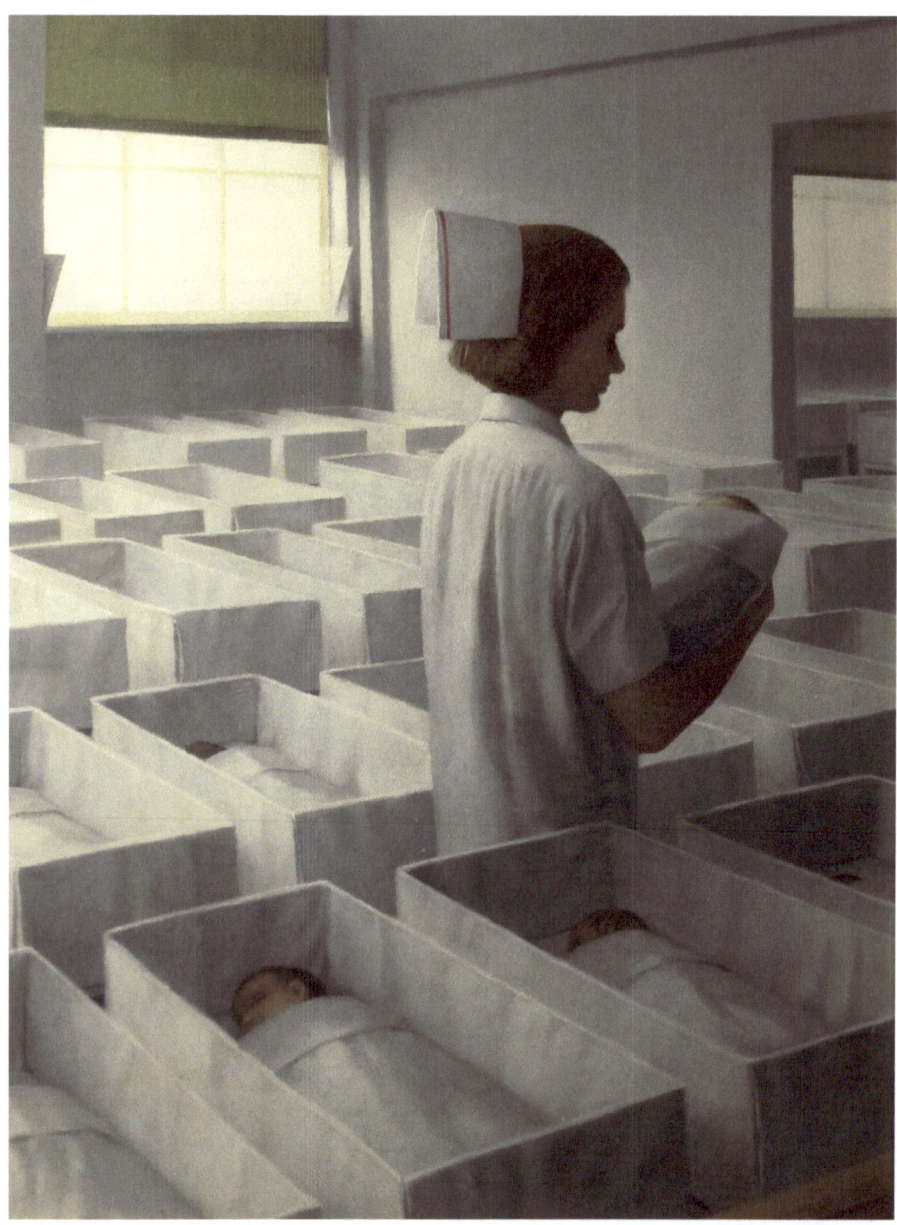

The Baby Boom, 1958
Proposed *Time* cover (never used)
Tempera on paperboard
16 x 12 inches
Harmon-Meek Gallery, Naples

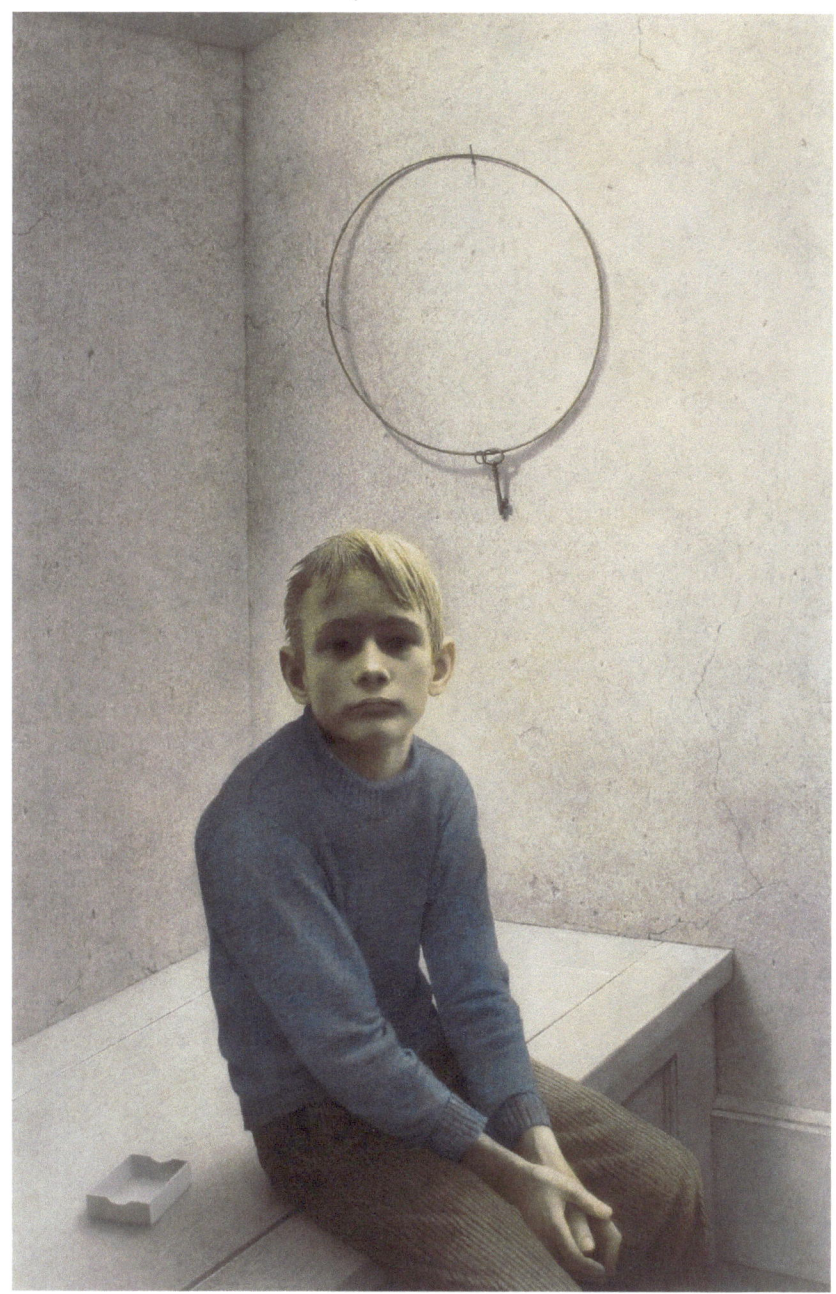

The Corner Seat, 1971
Egg tempera on gesso on masonite
36 x 24 inches
Harmon-Meek Gallery, Naples

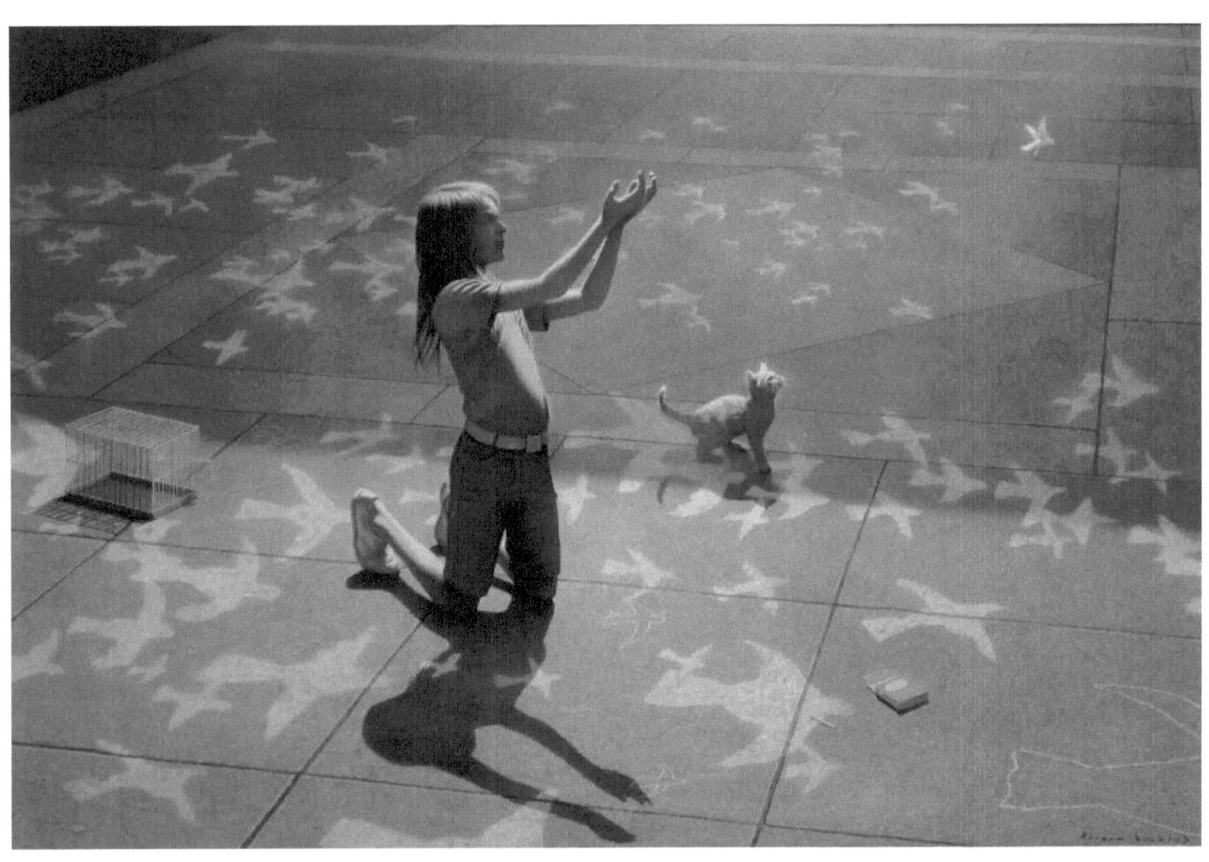

The Birdcage, 1972
Egg tempera on gesso on masonite
29 x 42 inches
Harmon-Meek Gallery, Naples

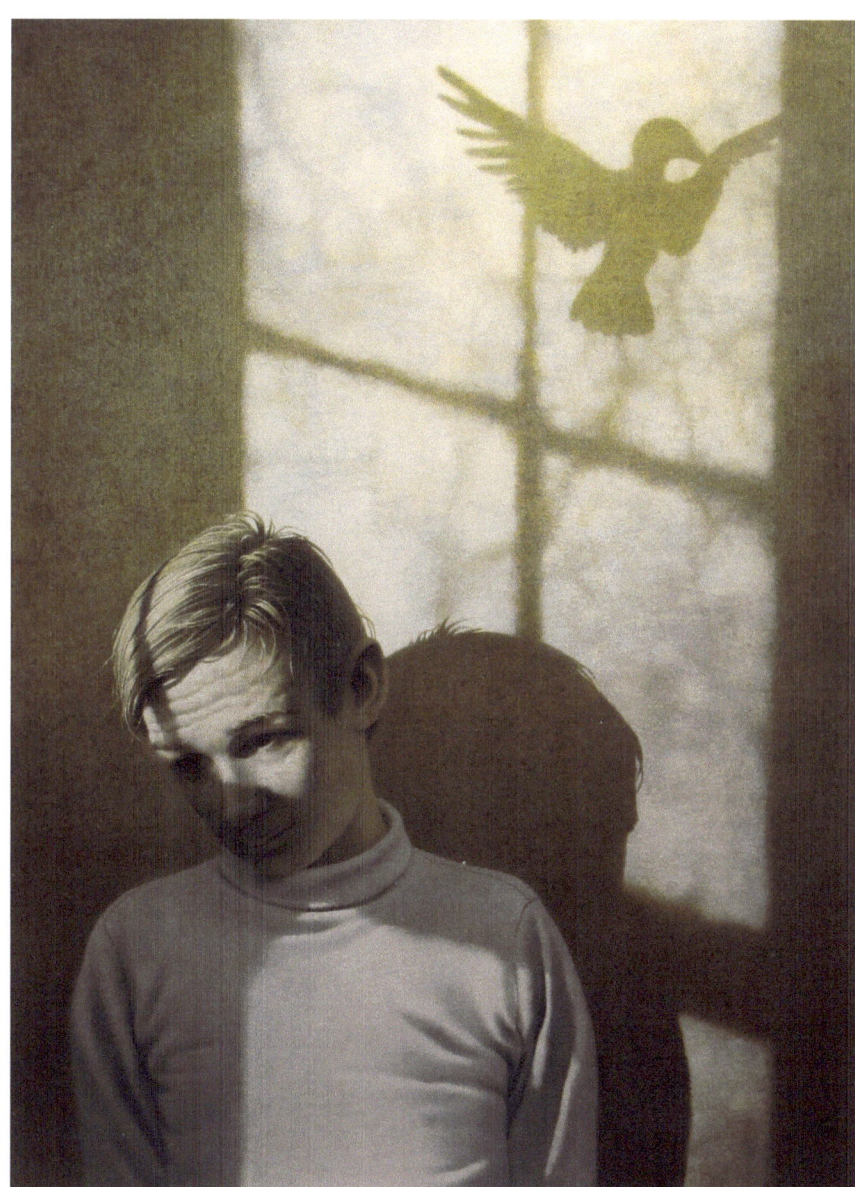

Bird at Window, 1972
Egg tempera on gesso on masonite
25 1/2 x 10 1/2 inches
Harmon-Meek Gallery, Naples

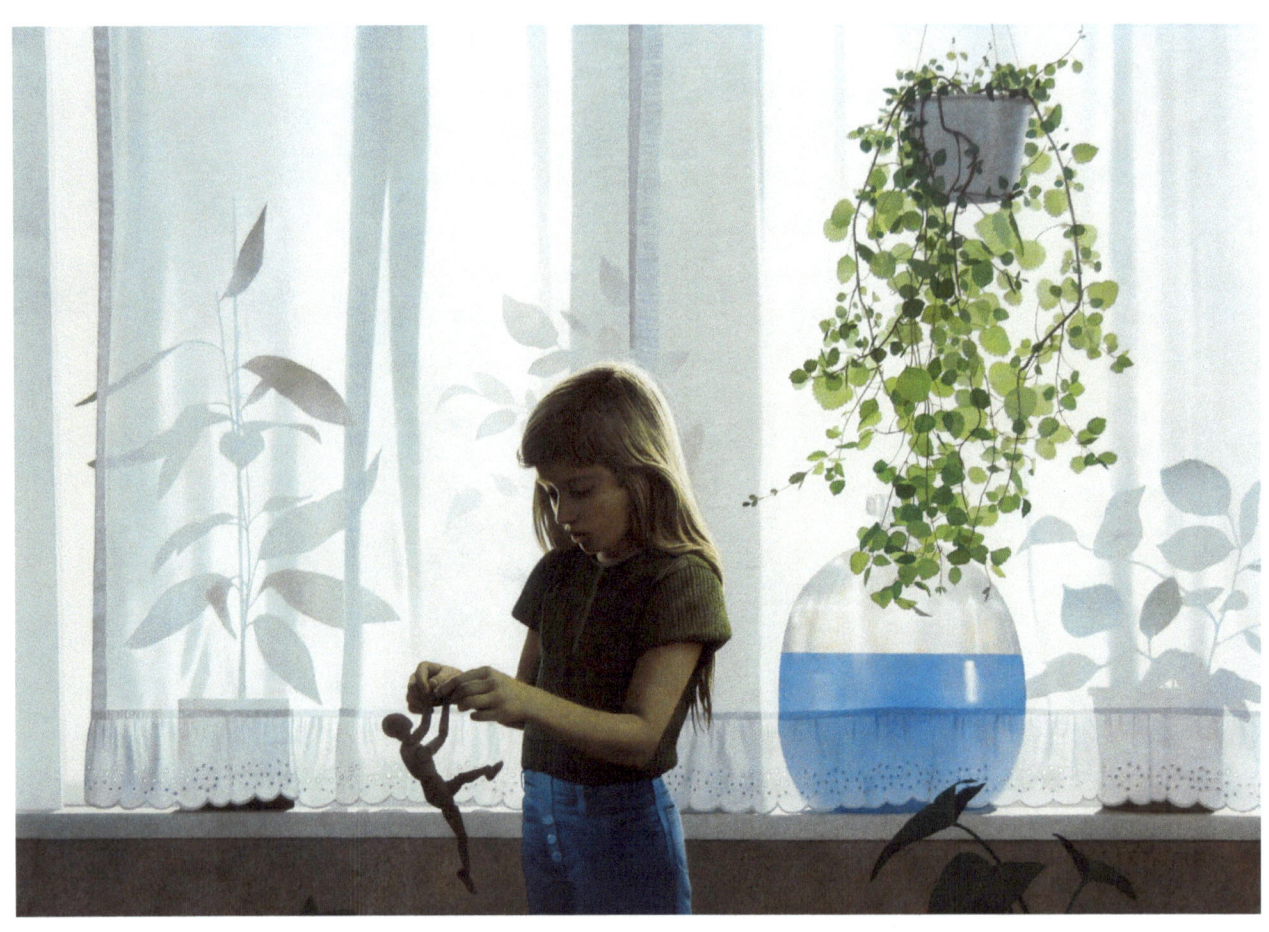

Manikin, 1975
Egg tempera on gesso on masonite
32 x 44 inches
William & Barbara Meek

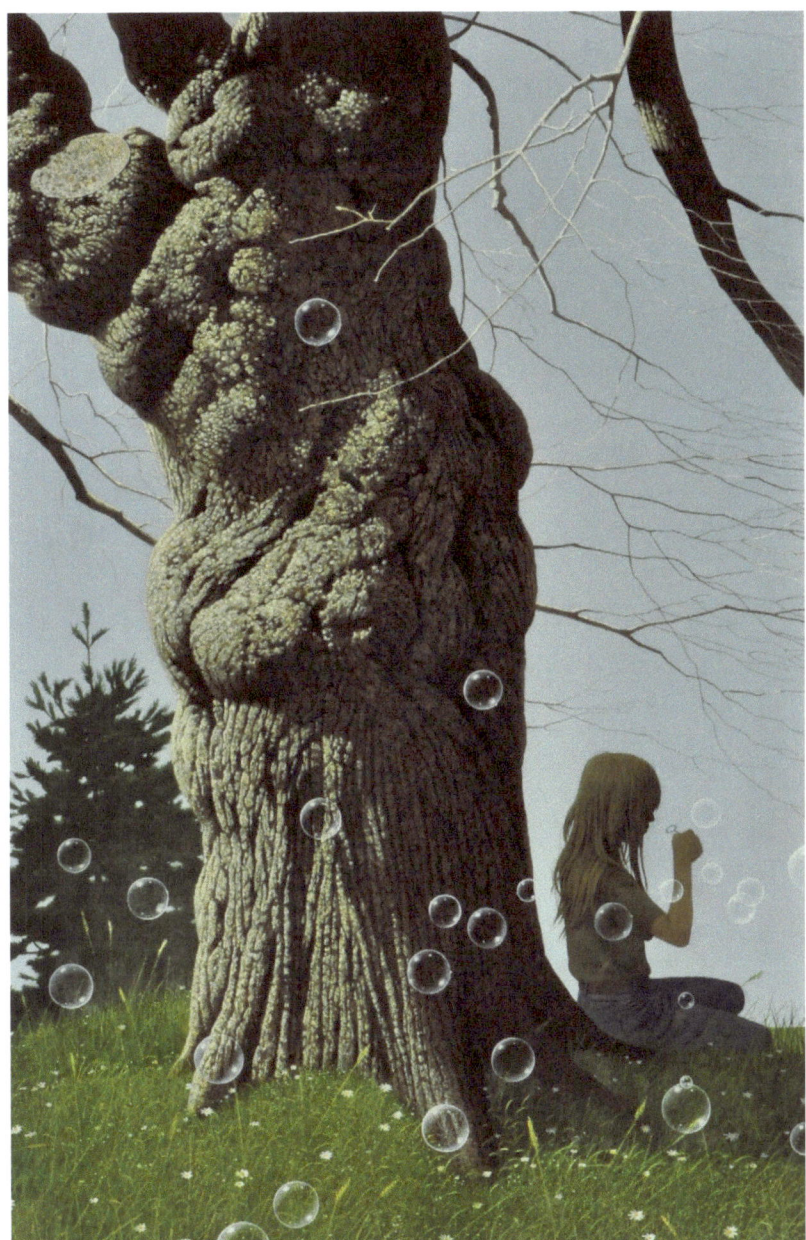

Old Mulberry, 1976
Egg tempera on gesso on masonite
30 x 20 inches
Harmon-Meek Gallery, Naples

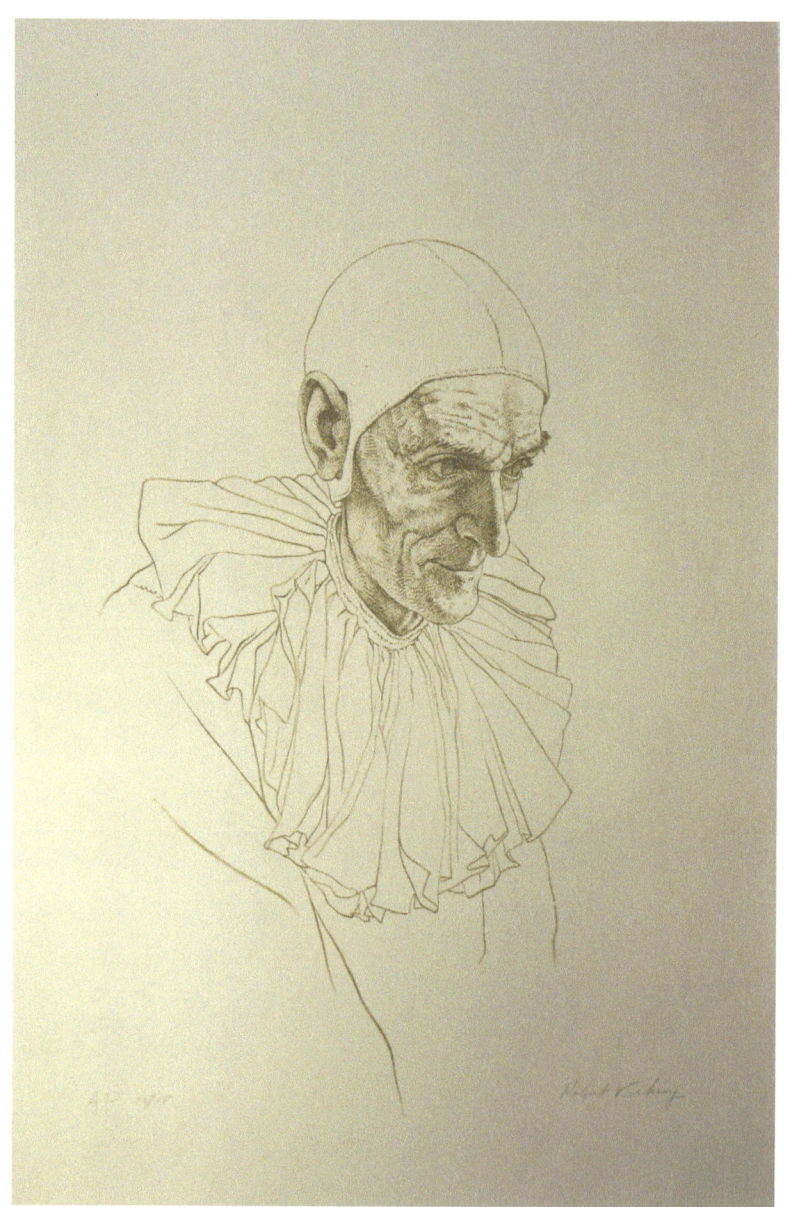

Clown with Ruff, 1977
Lithograph (edition of 150)
30 x 22 inches
Harmon-Meek Gallery, Naples

Melvin Art Gallery | ROBERT VICKREY: *Master of Magic Realism*

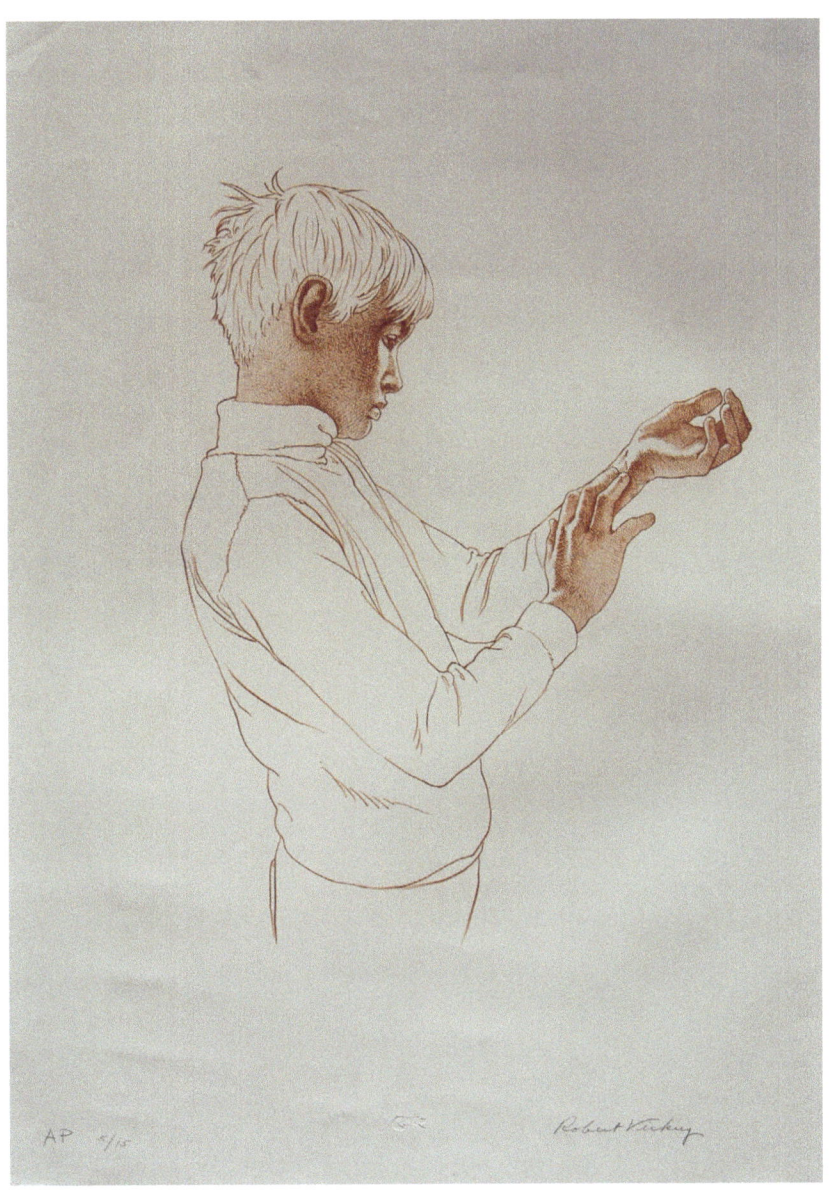

AP 5/15 Robert Vickrey

Sean's Pulse, 1977
Lithograph (edition of 150)
30 x 22 inches
Harmon-Meek Gallery, Naples

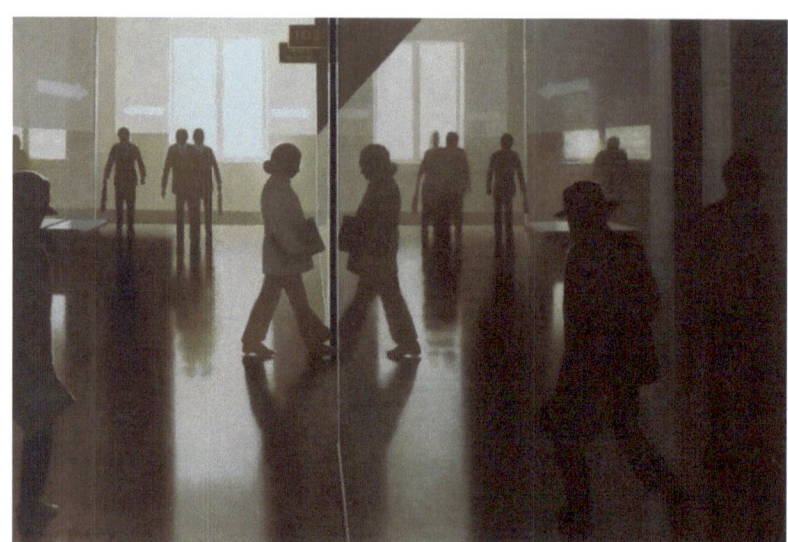

Corridors of the Law, 1983
Oil on masonite
25 x 38 inches
Juliana Meek

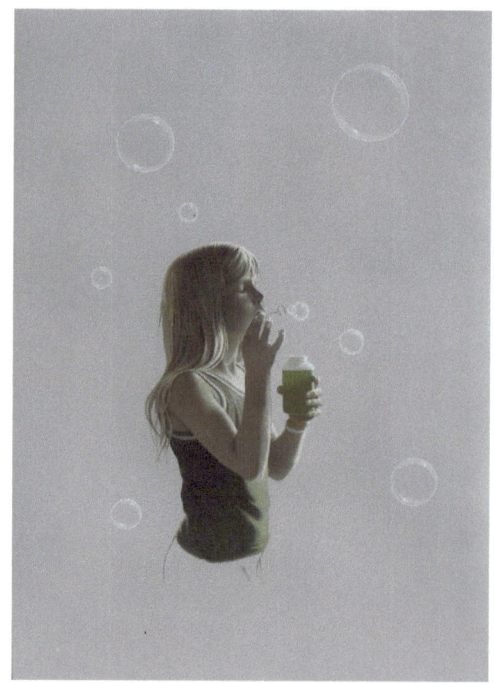

Study for Bubble Play, 1984
Acrylic on paperboard
39 x 29 inches
Harmon-Meek Gallery, Naples

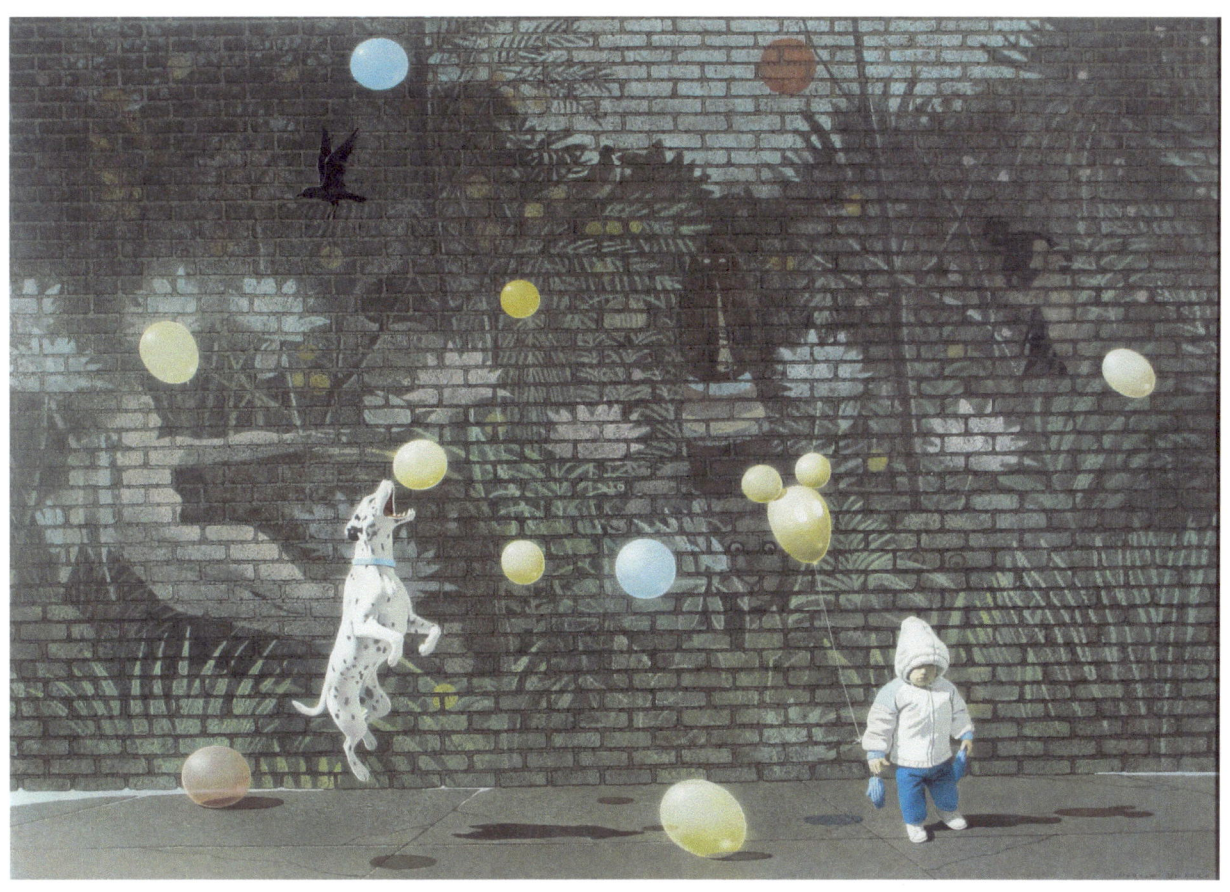

Midwinter Dreams, 1984
Egg tempera on gesso on masonite
35 1/2 x 47 inches
Harmon-Meek Gallery, Naples

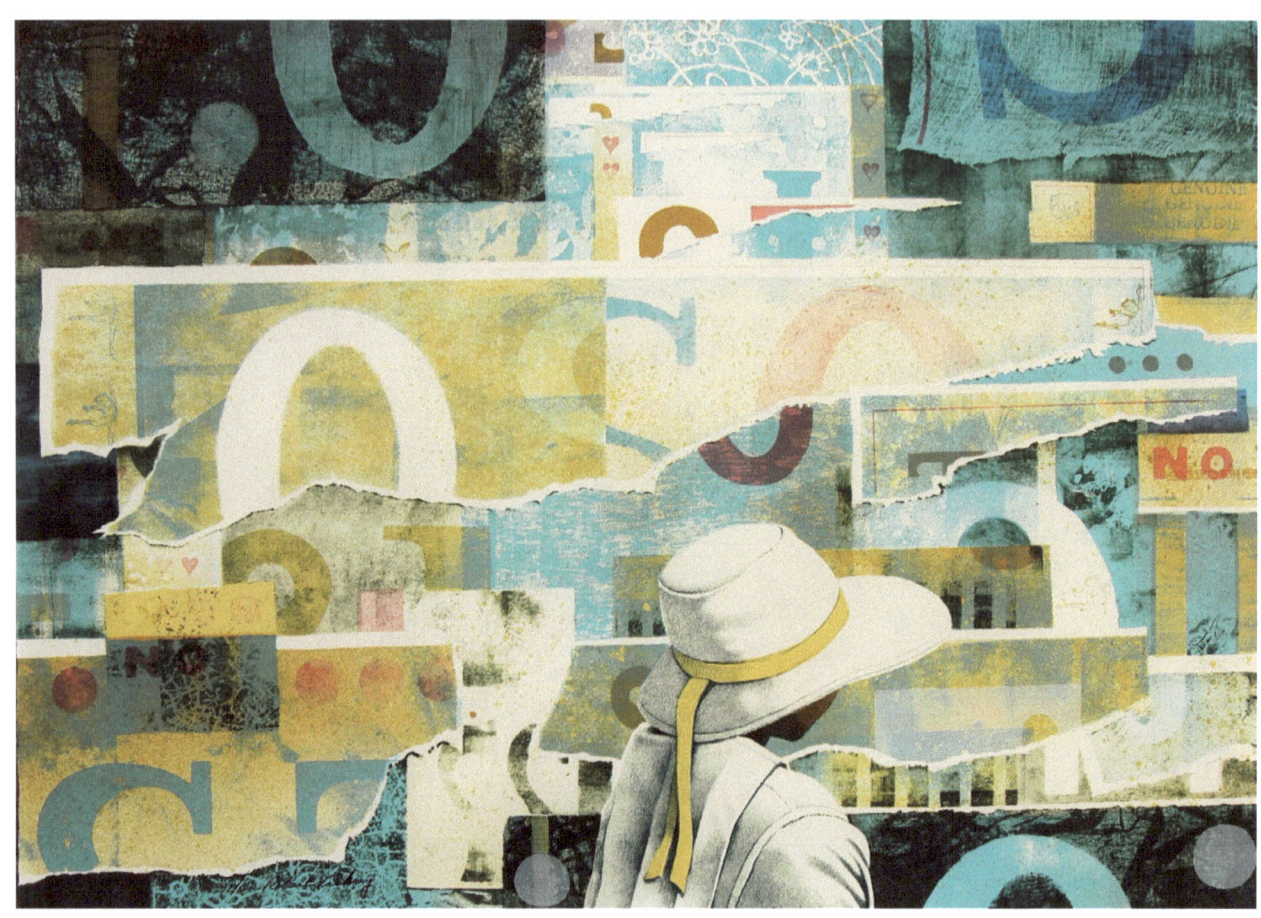

Poster Wall, 1984
Lithograph (edition of 100)
22 x 30 inches
Harmon-Meek Gallery, Naples

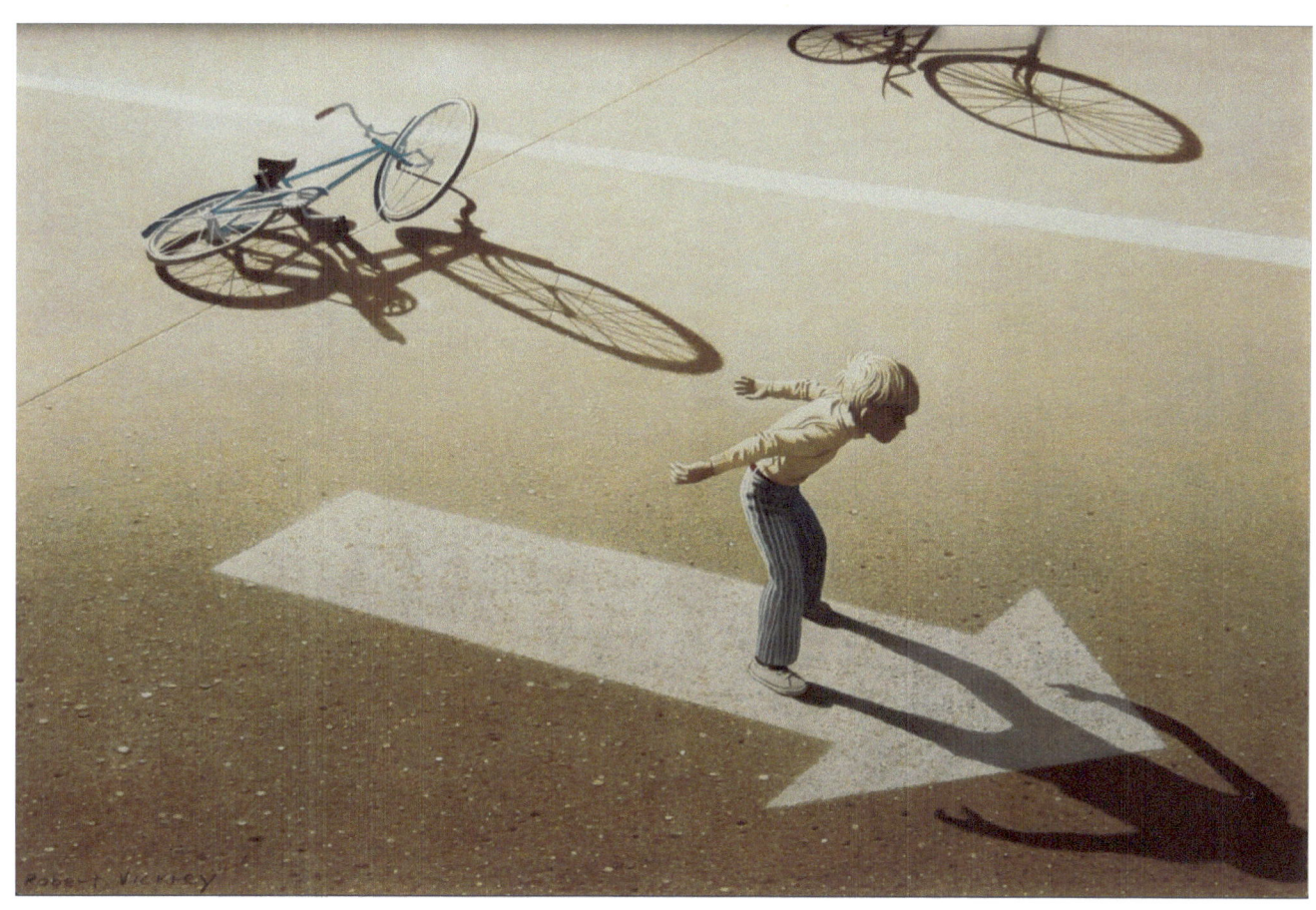

Street Surfer, 1986
Egg tempera on gesso on masonite
16 x 23 inches
William & Barbara Meek

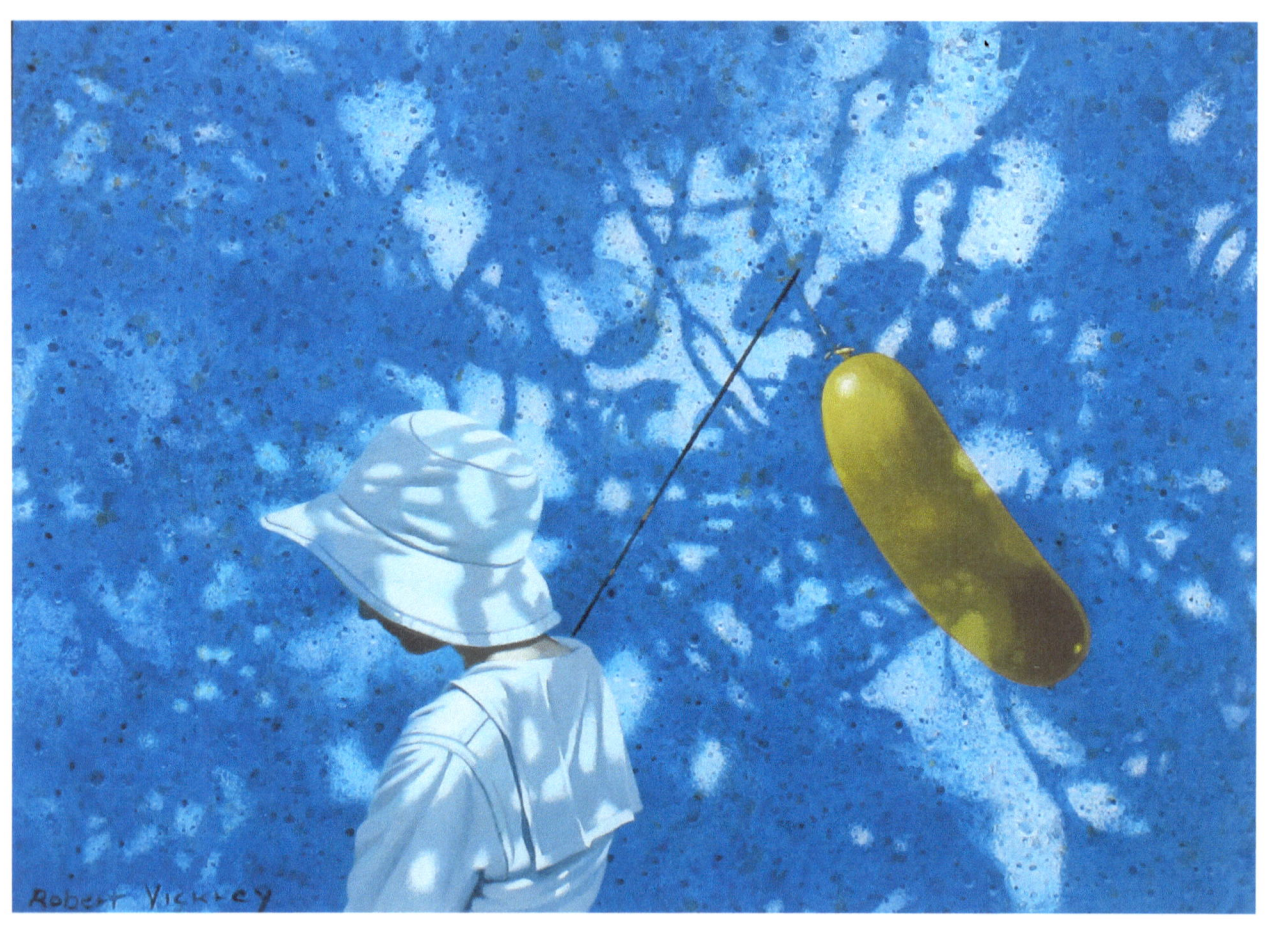

Caroline's Sailor Suit, 1987
Acrylic on masonite
12 x 16 inches
Harmon-Meek Gallery, Naples

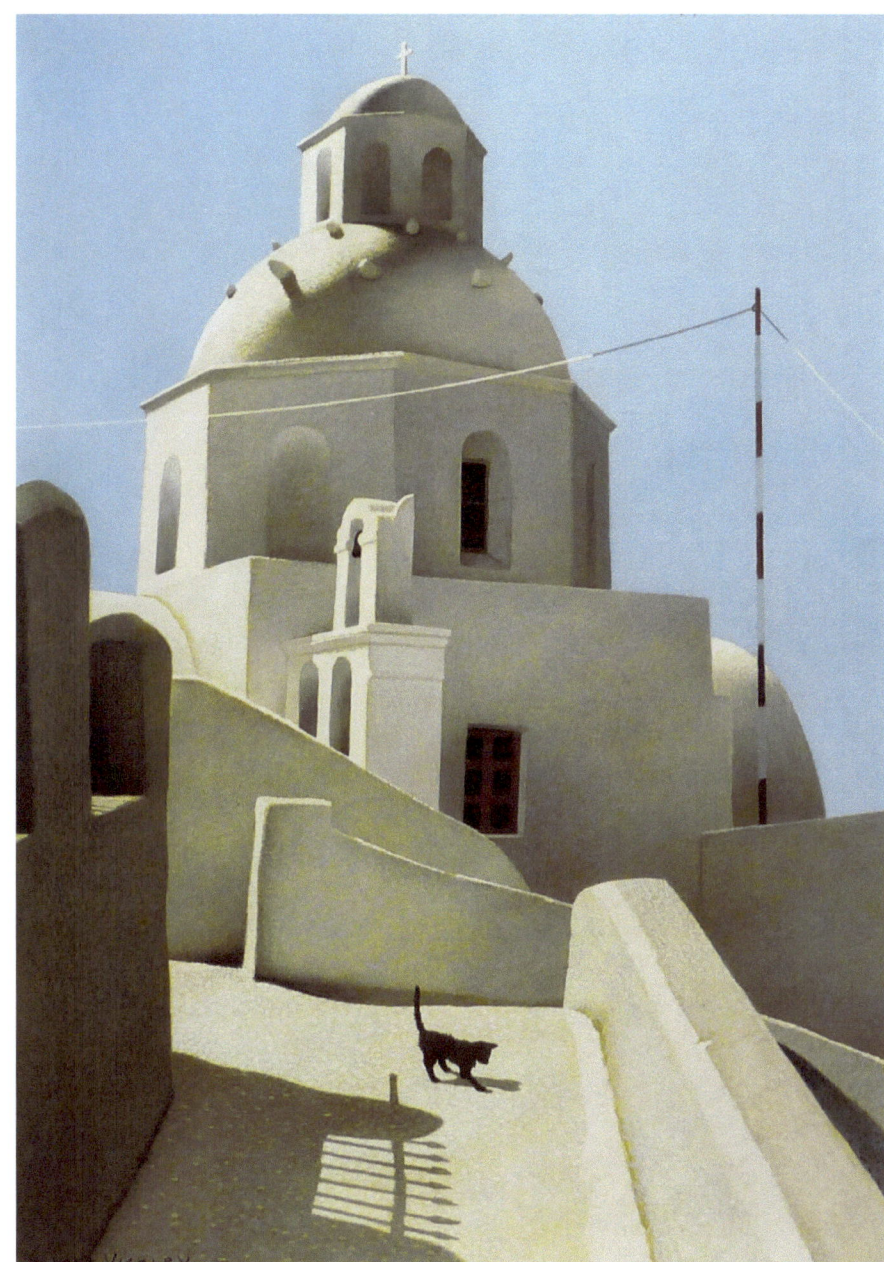

Santorini Chapel, 1986
Egg tempera on gesso on masonite
20 x 16 inches
Robert Wenzel

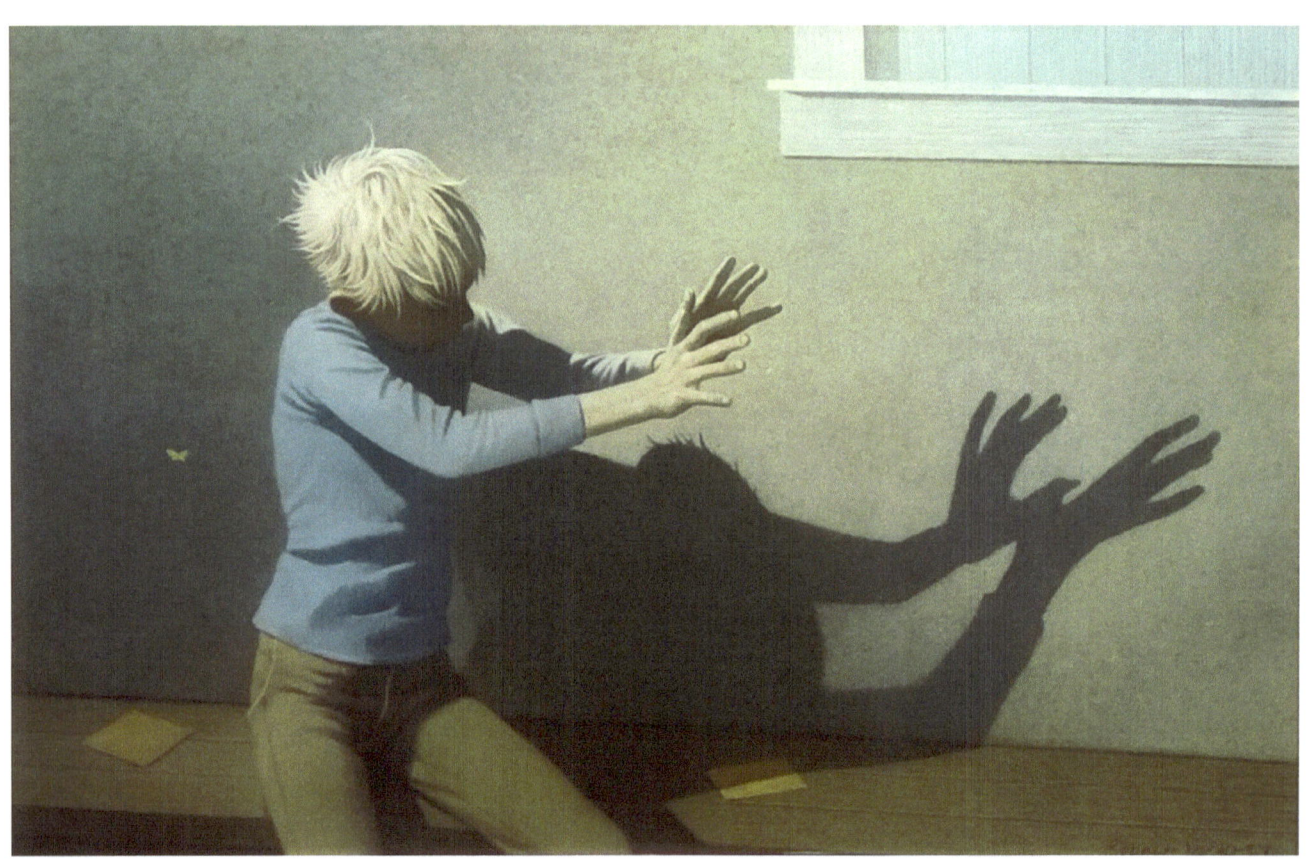

Bird in Flight, 1988
Oil on paperboard
17 3/4 x 26 1/2 inches
Harmon-Meek Gallery, Naples

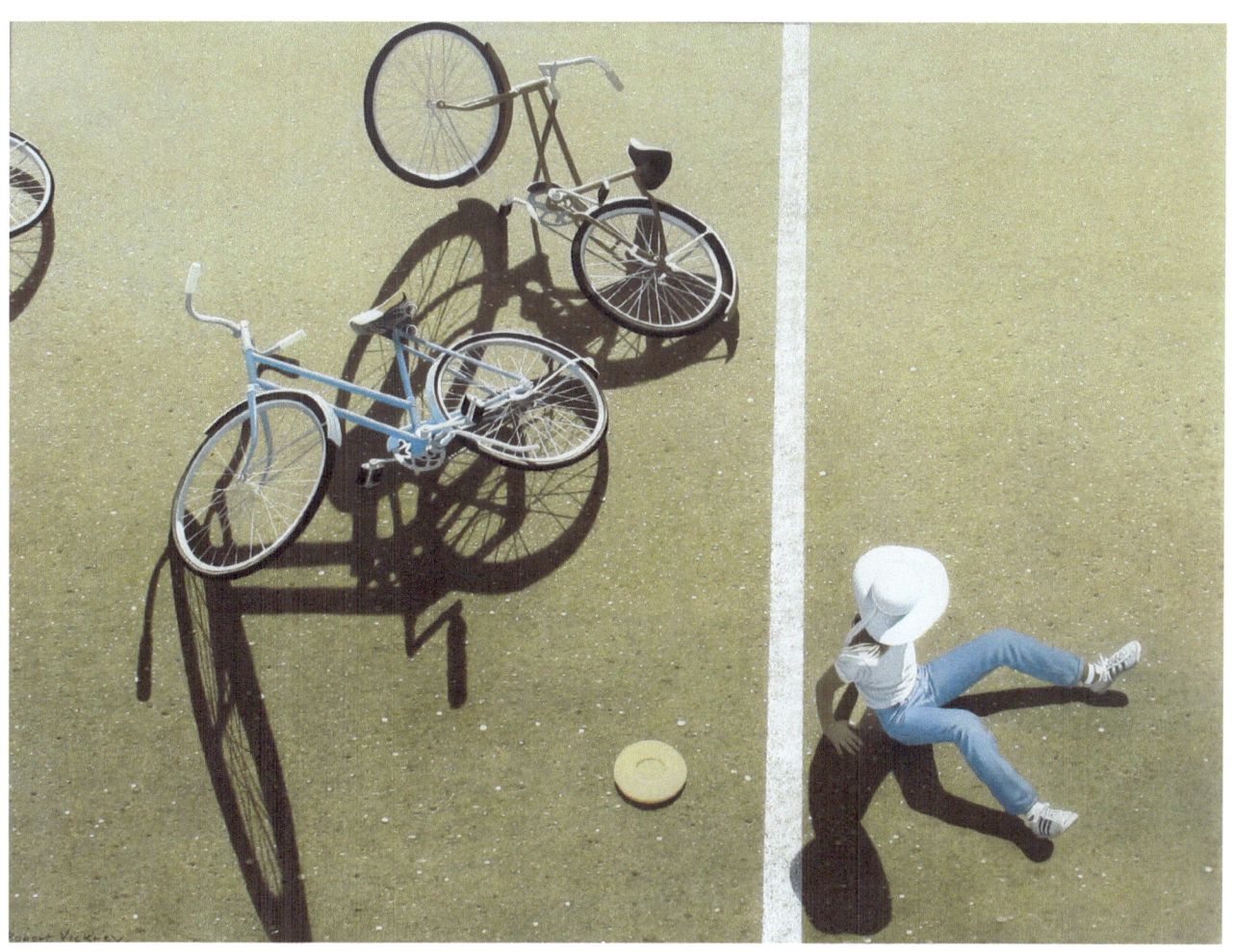

Kim From Above, 1988
Egg tempera on gesso on masonite
30 x 40 inches
Harmon-Meek Gallery, Naples

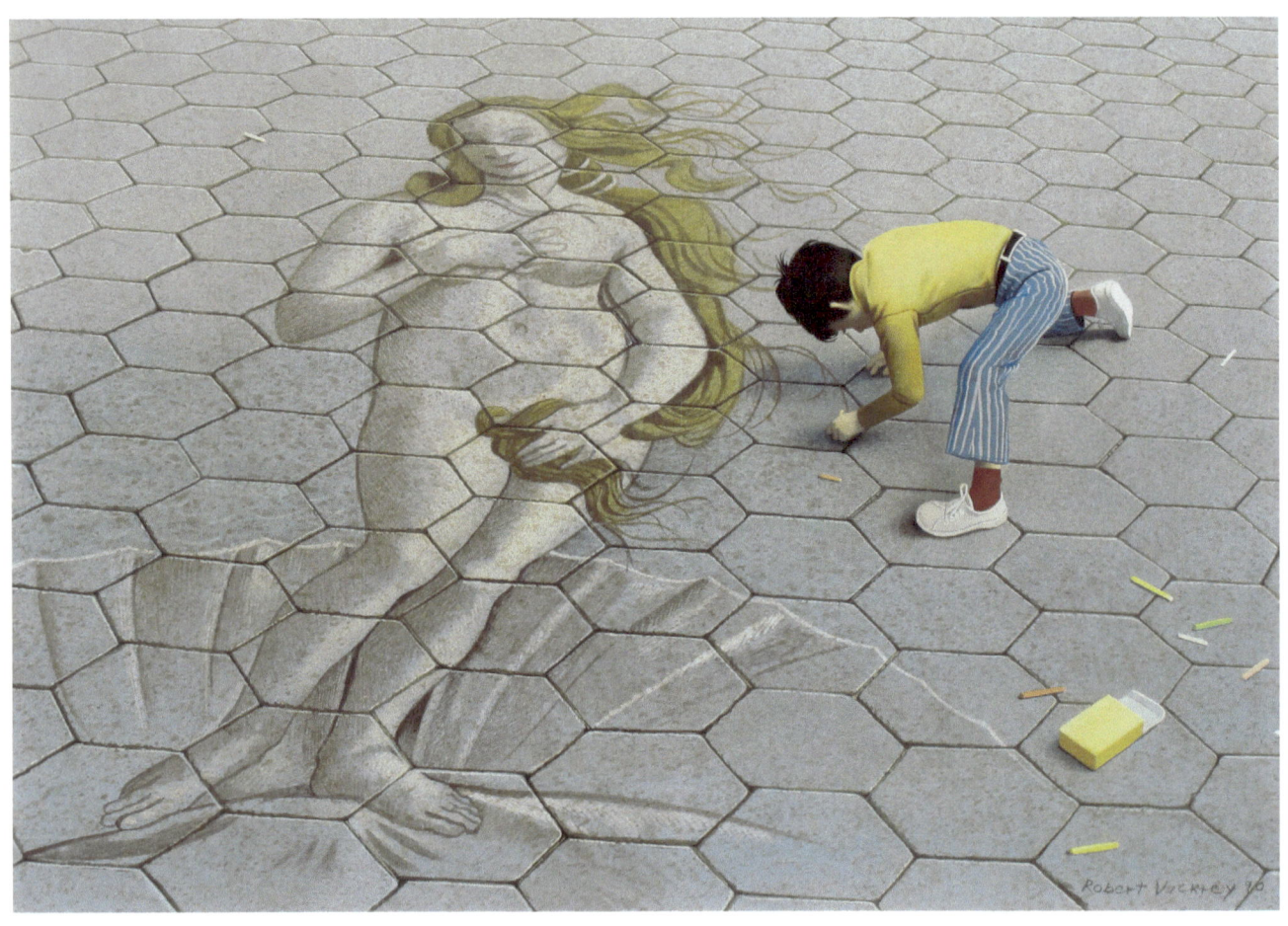

Clam's Eye View 1990
Egg tempera on gesso on masonite
18 1/2 x 26 inches
William & Barbara Meek

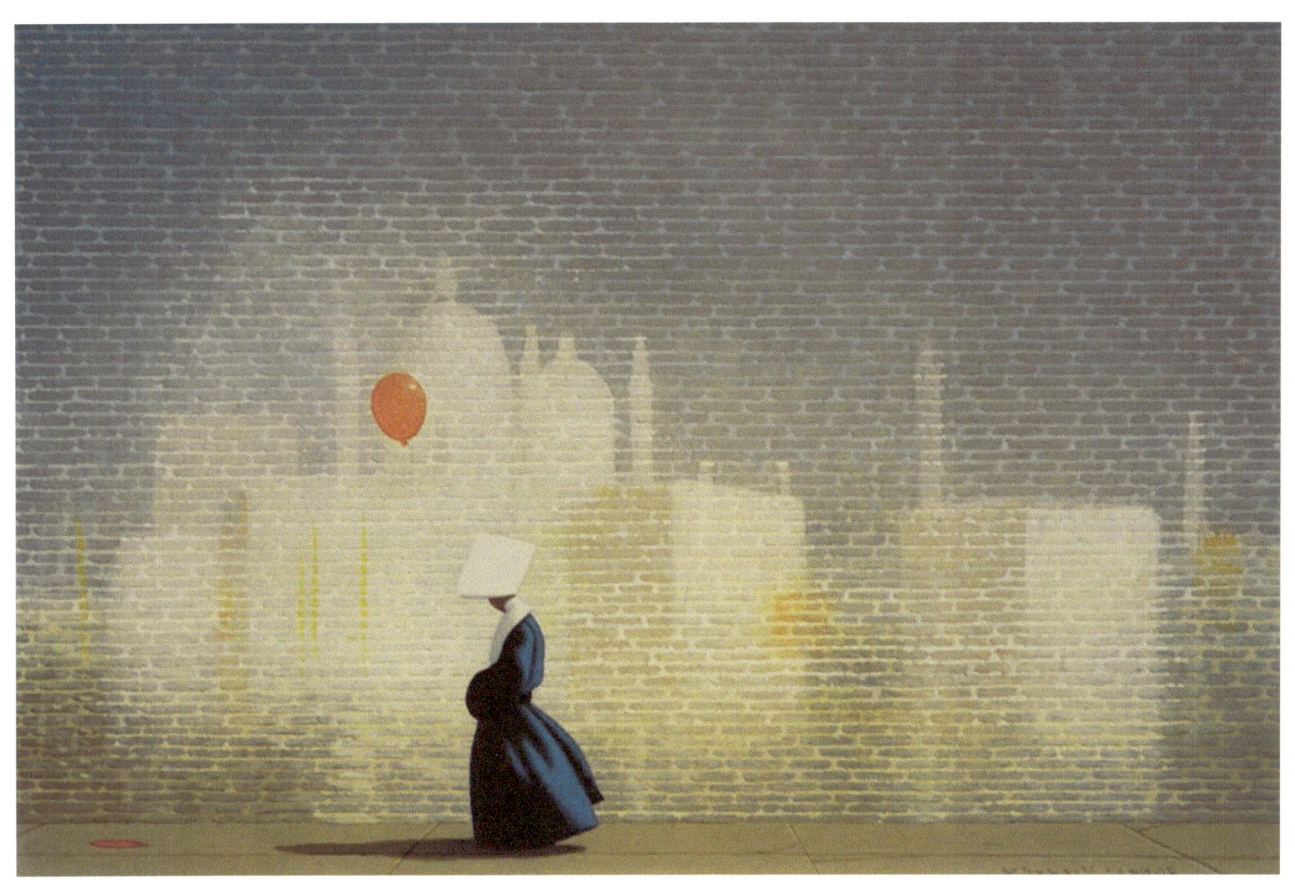

Venetian Dream, 1990
Egg tempera on gesso on masonite
8 1/2 x 12 inches
William & Barbara Meek

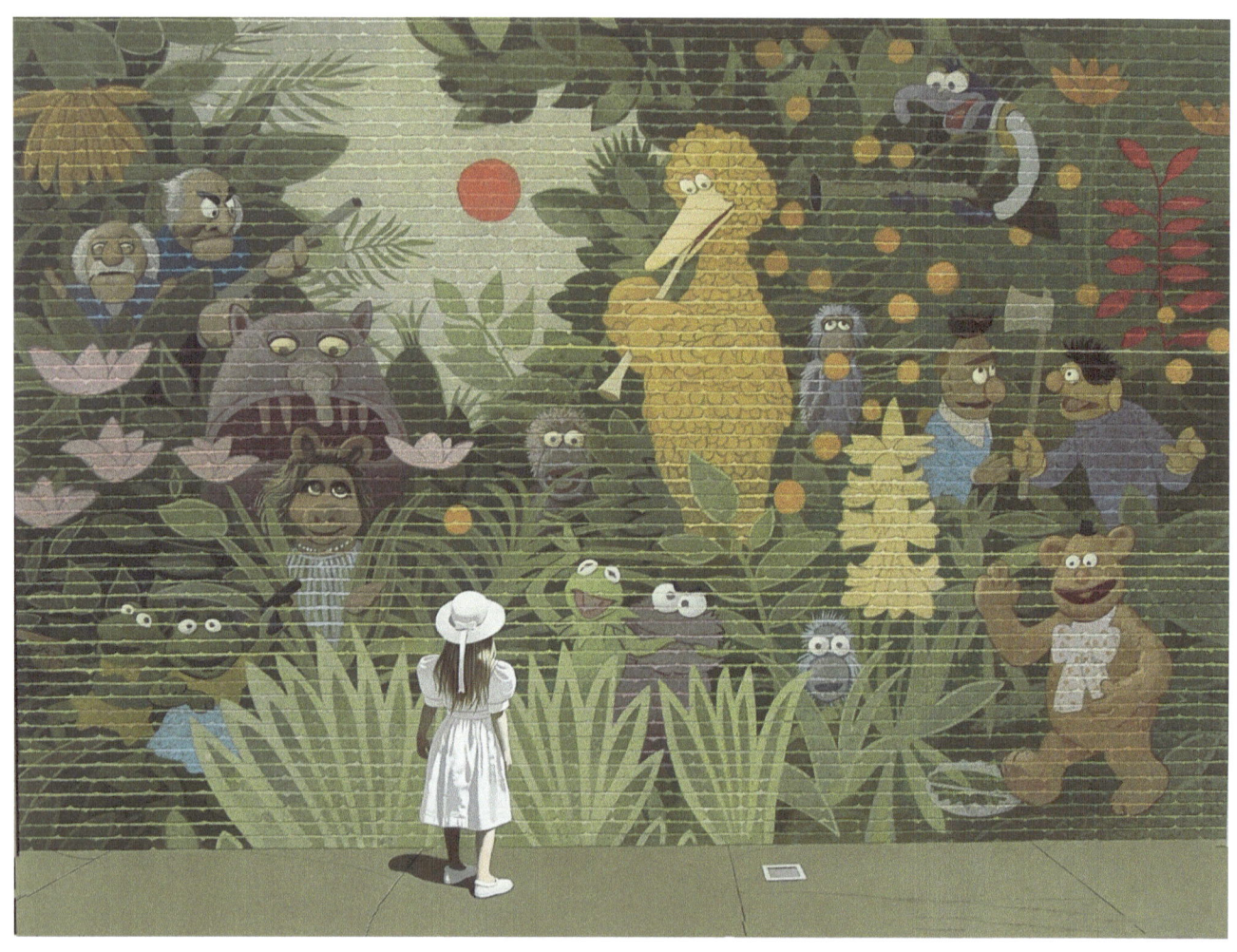

Lacy's Jungle, 1993
Egg tempera on gesso on masonite
36 x 38 inches
Harmon-Meek Gallery, Naples

Melvin Art Gallery | ROBERT VICKREY: *Master of Magic Realism*

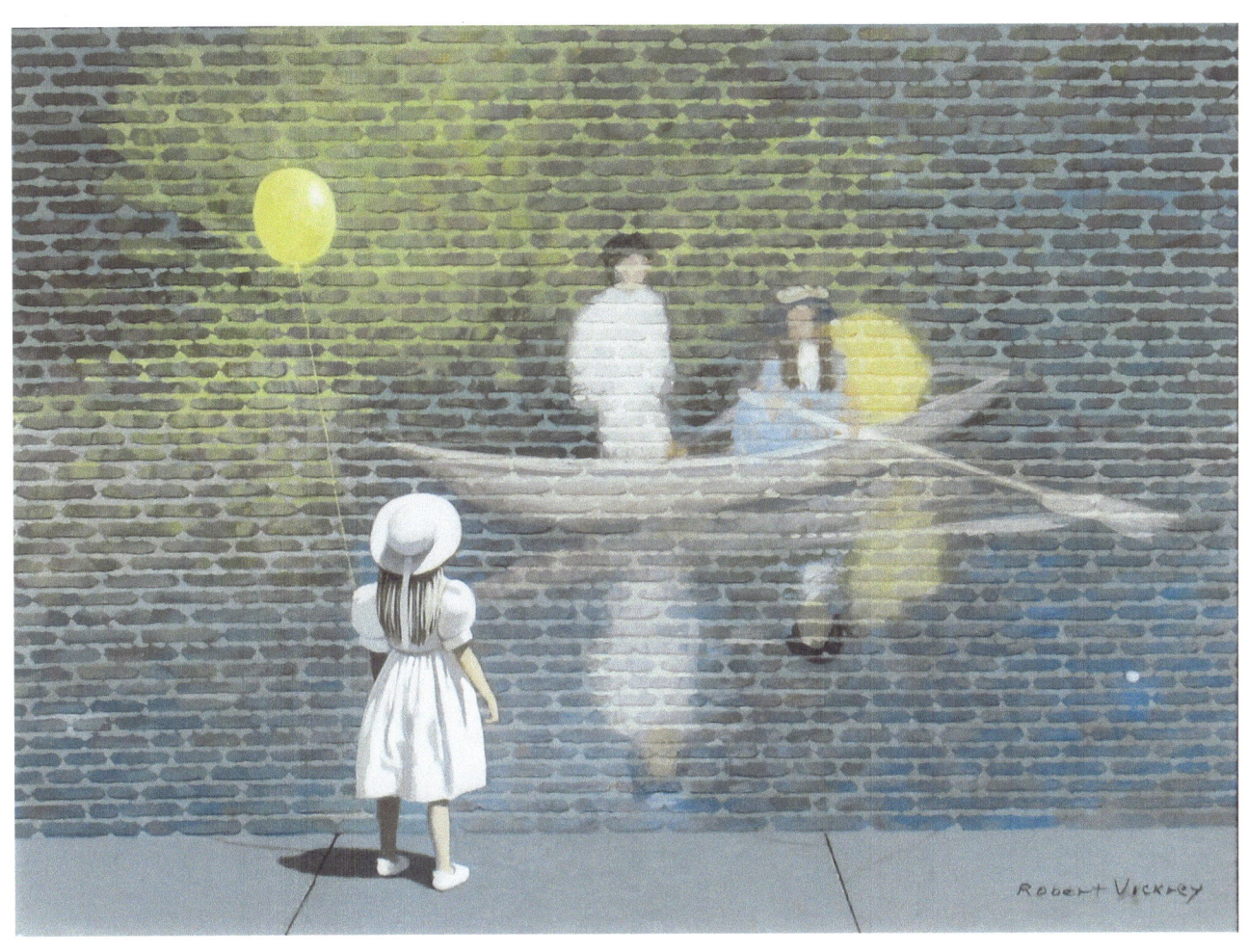

Boating Party, 1994
Egg tempera on gesso on masonite
9 x 12 inches
Harmon-Meek Gallery, Naples

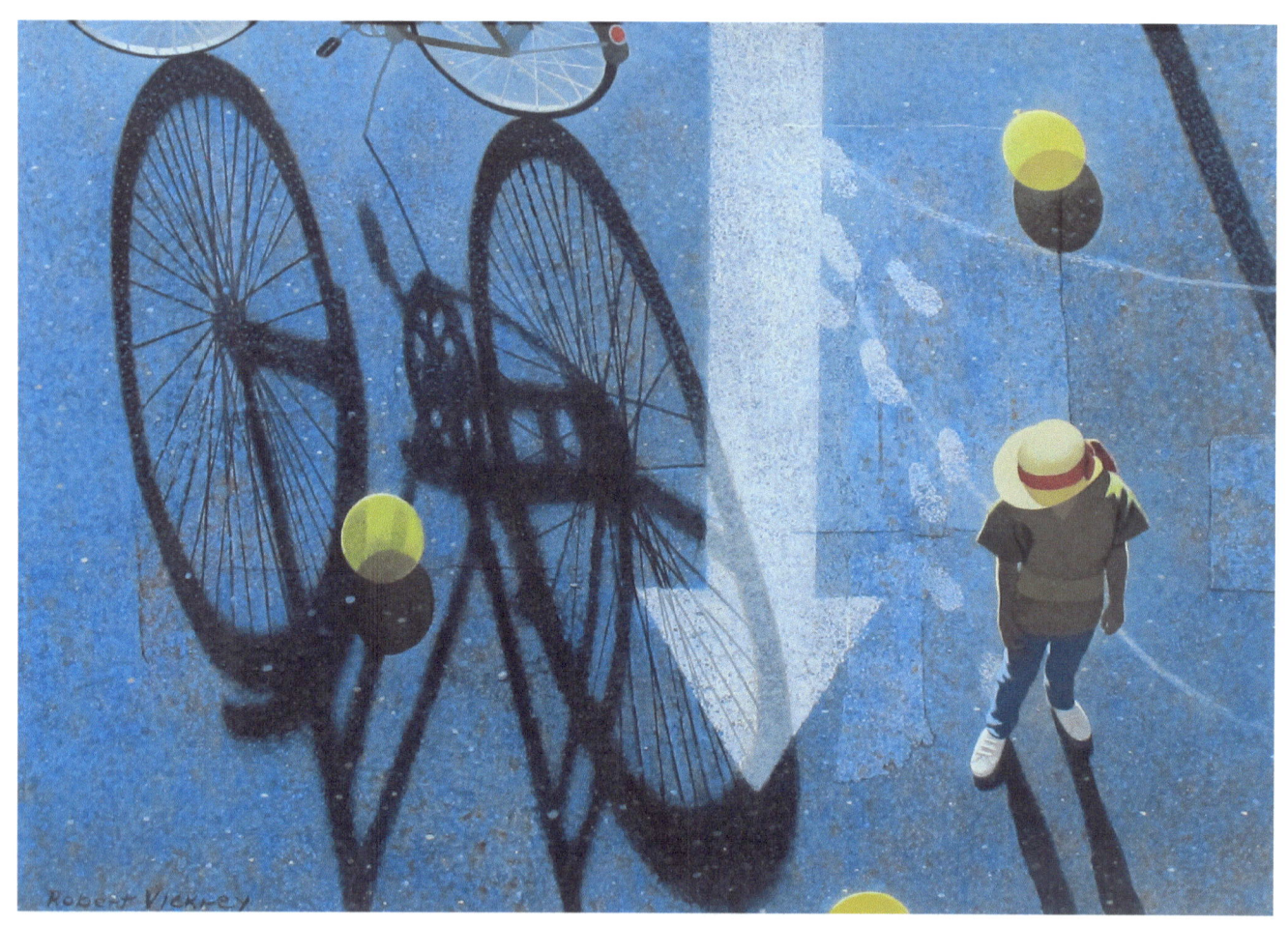

Lacy's Footprints, 1994
Egg tempera on gesso on masonite
13 1/2 x 18 1/2 inches
Harmon-Meek Gallery, Naples

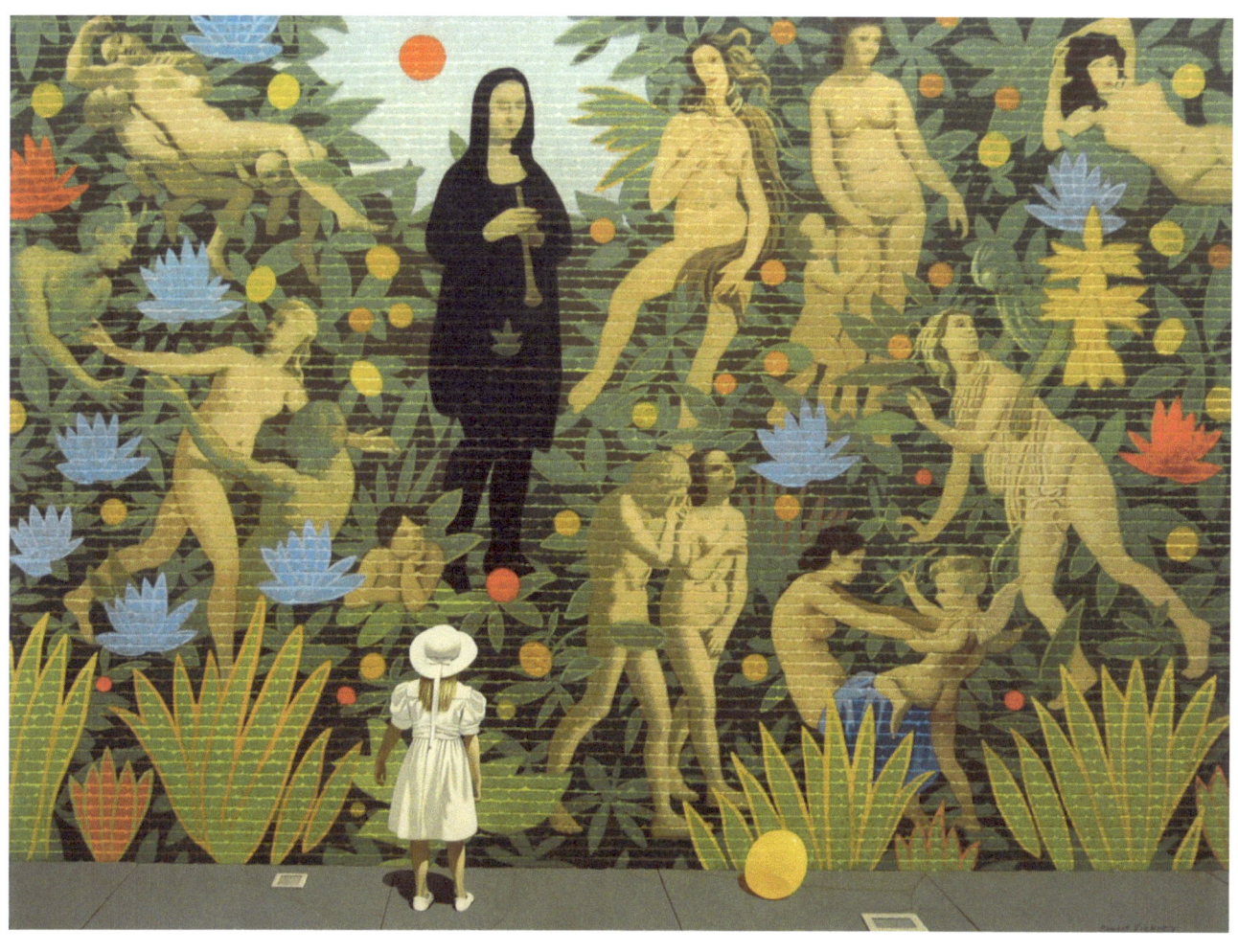

Forbidden Fruit, 1995
Egg tempera on gesso on masonite
36 x 48 inches
Harmon-Meek Gallery, Naples

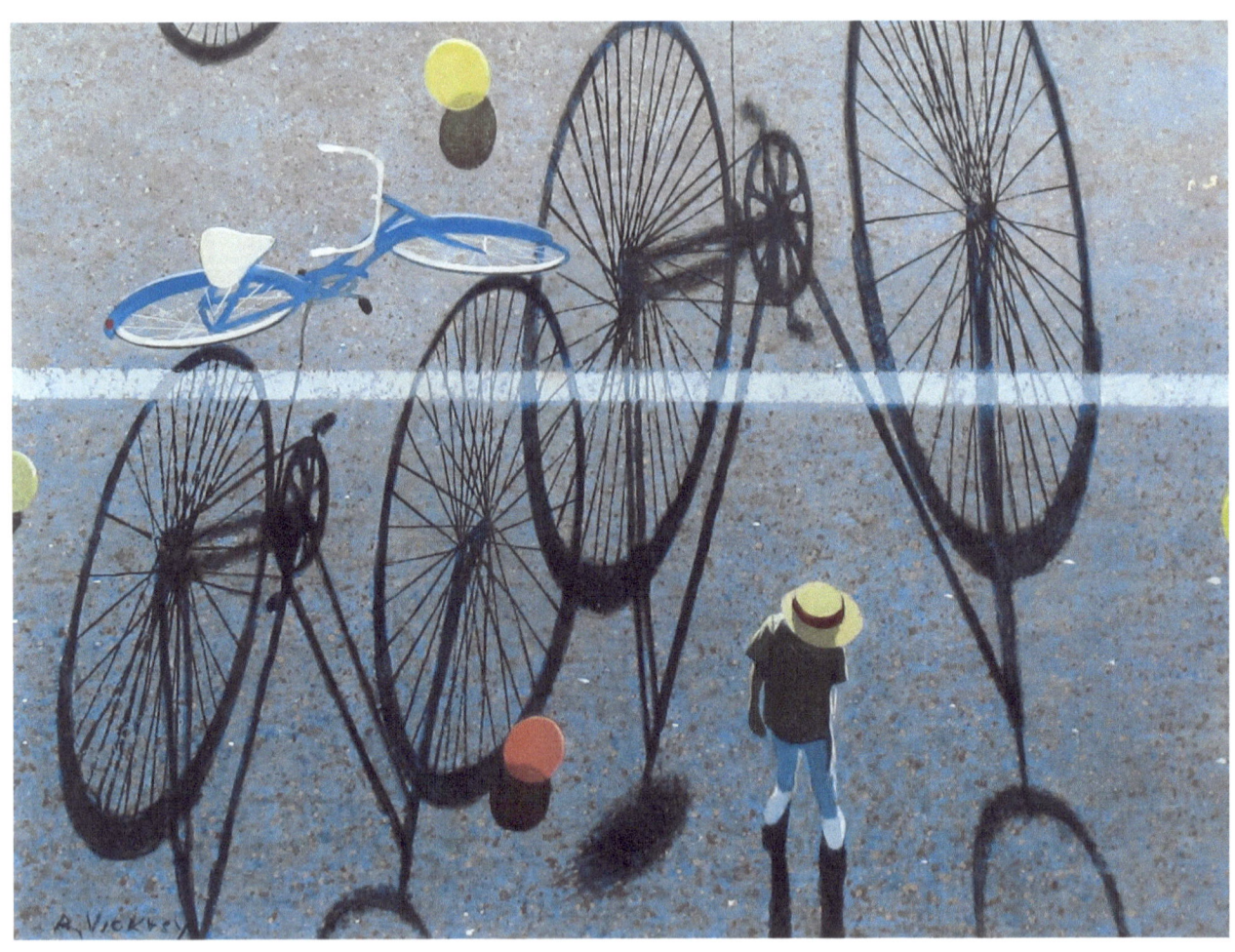

Red , Yellow & Green, 1995
Egg tempera on gesso on masonite
7 1/4 x 9 inches
Harmon-Meek Gallery, Naples

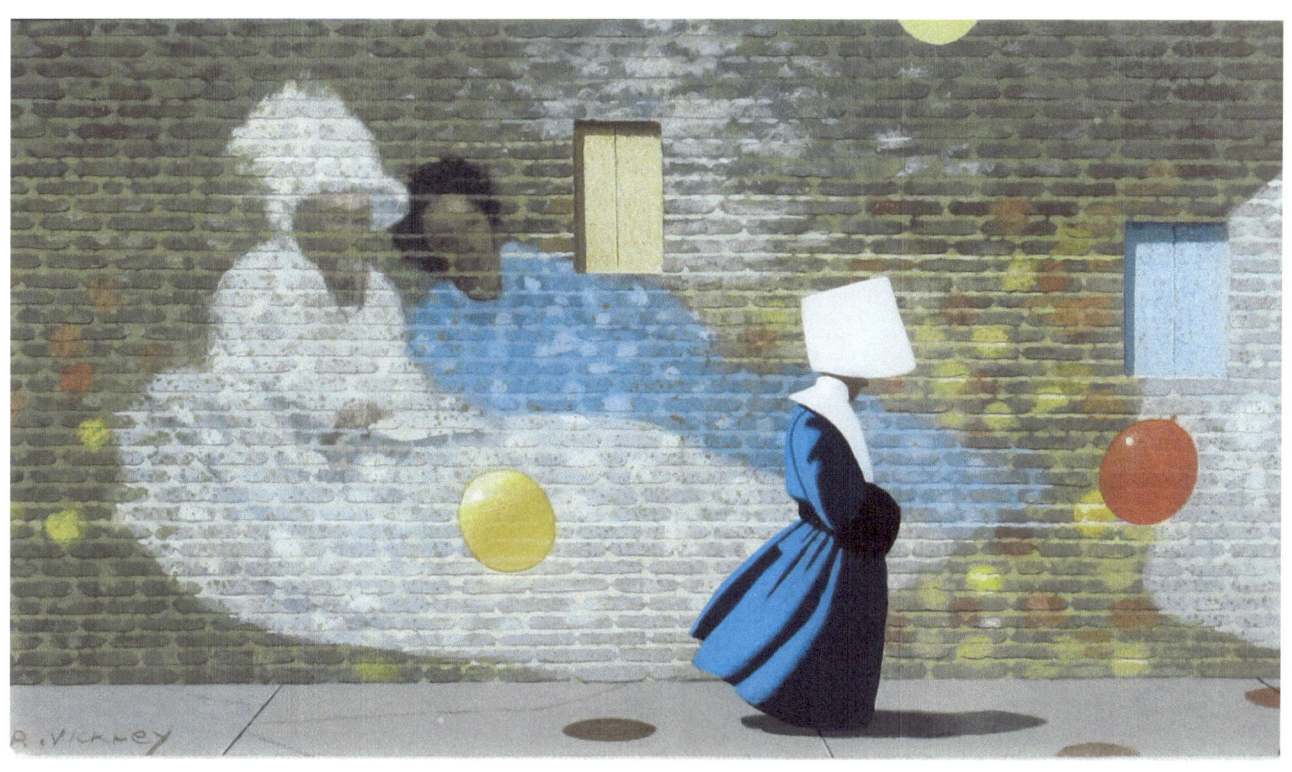

Monet's Gossips, 1995
Egg tempera on gesso on masonite
7 x 12 inches
Harmon-Meek Gallery, Naples

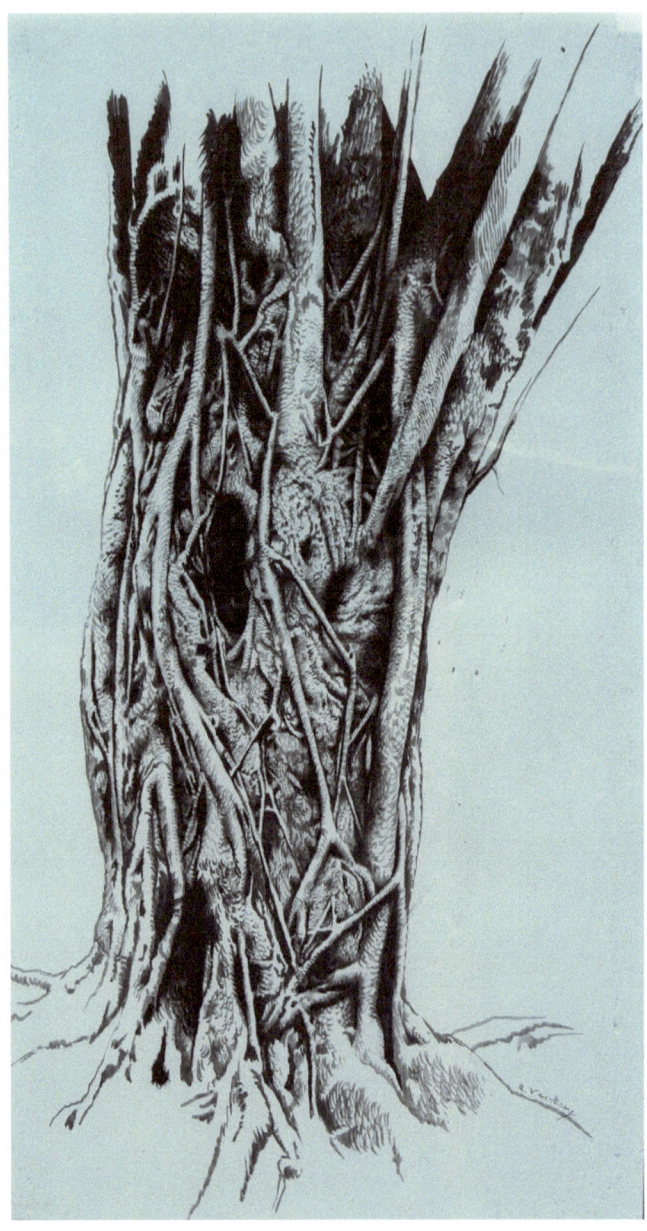

First Banyon Study, 1995
Ink
32 x 22 inches
Harmon-Meek Gallery, Naples

Melvin Art Gallery | ROBERT VICKREY: *Master of Magic Realism*

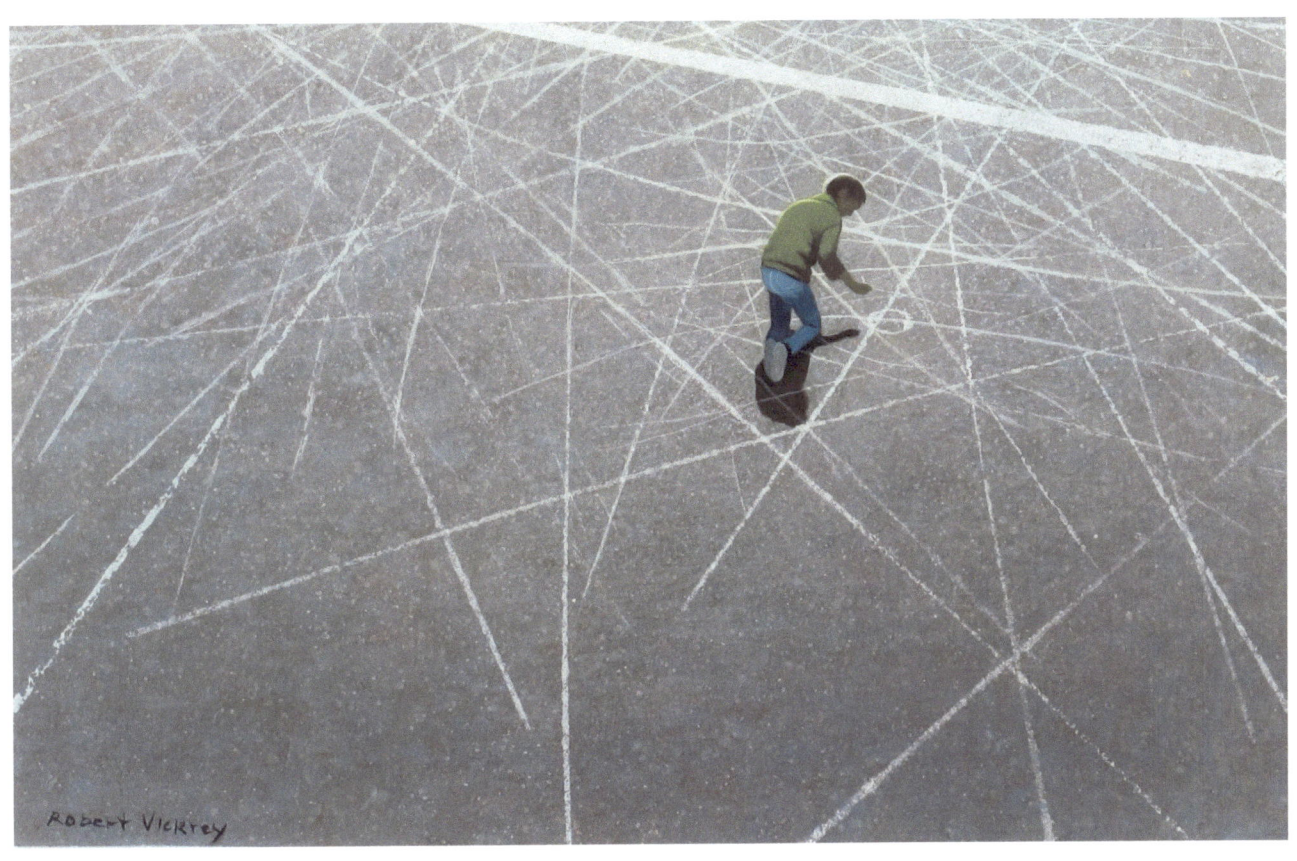

Intersections, 1996
Egg tempera on gesso on masonite
8 x 12 inches
Harmon-Meek Gallery, Naples

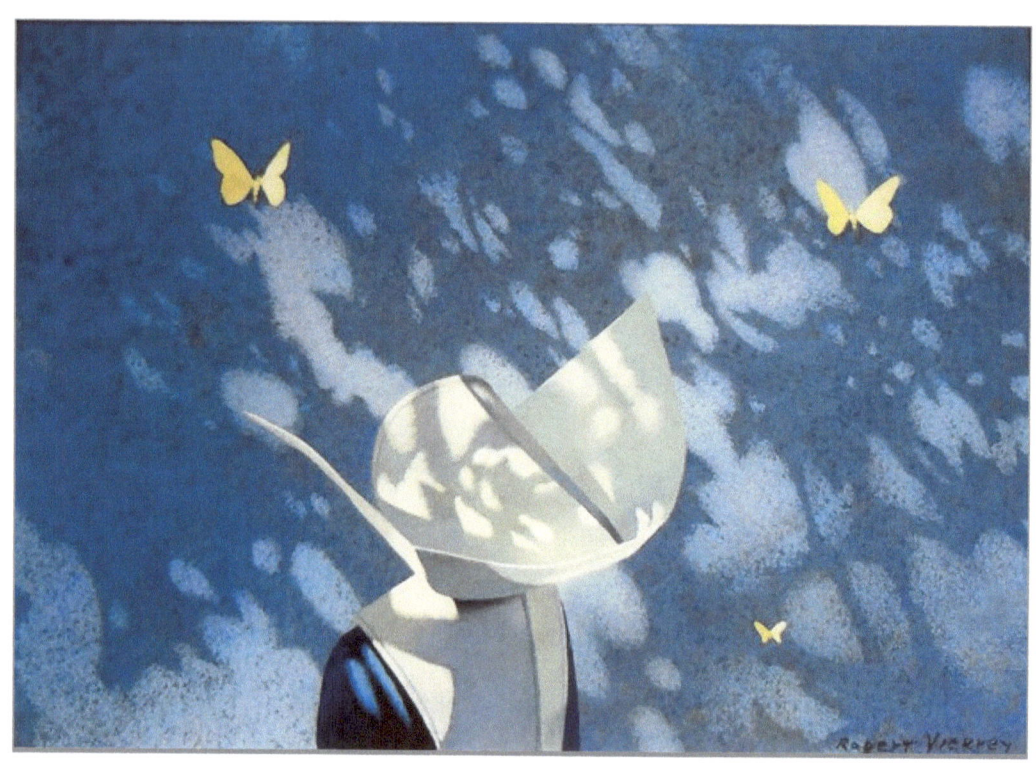

Monarch Triumvirate, 1996
Egg tempera on gesso on masonite
11 1/2 x 16 inches
Harmon-Meek Gallery, Naples

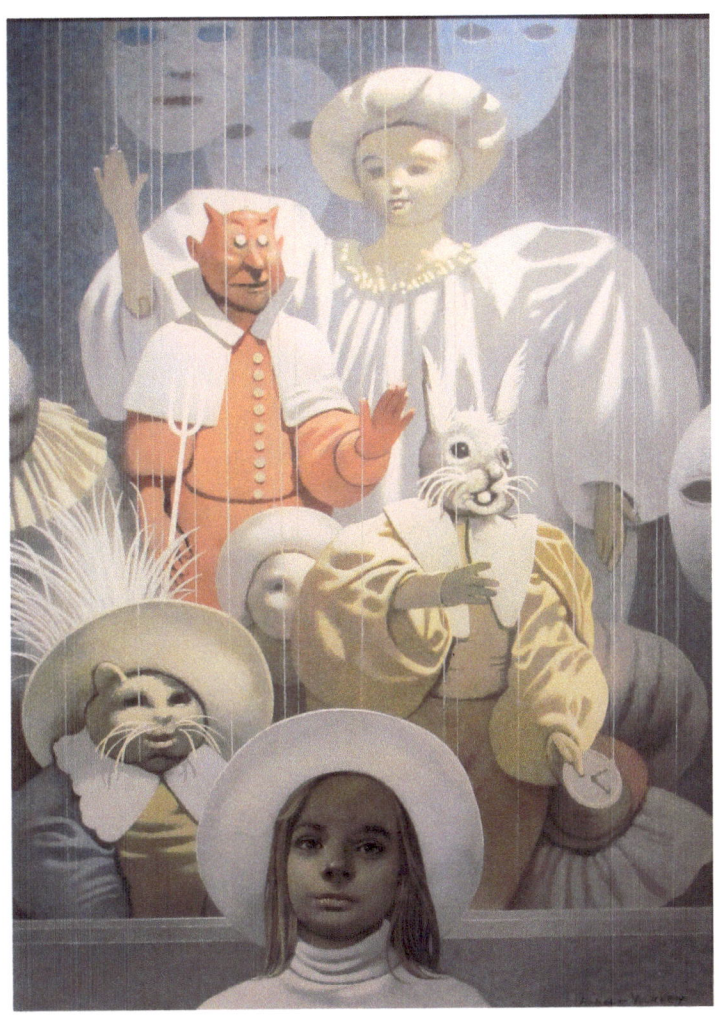

Masks & Marionette, 2000
Egg tempera on gesso on masonite
23 x 15 3/4 inches
Harmon-Meek Gallery, Naples

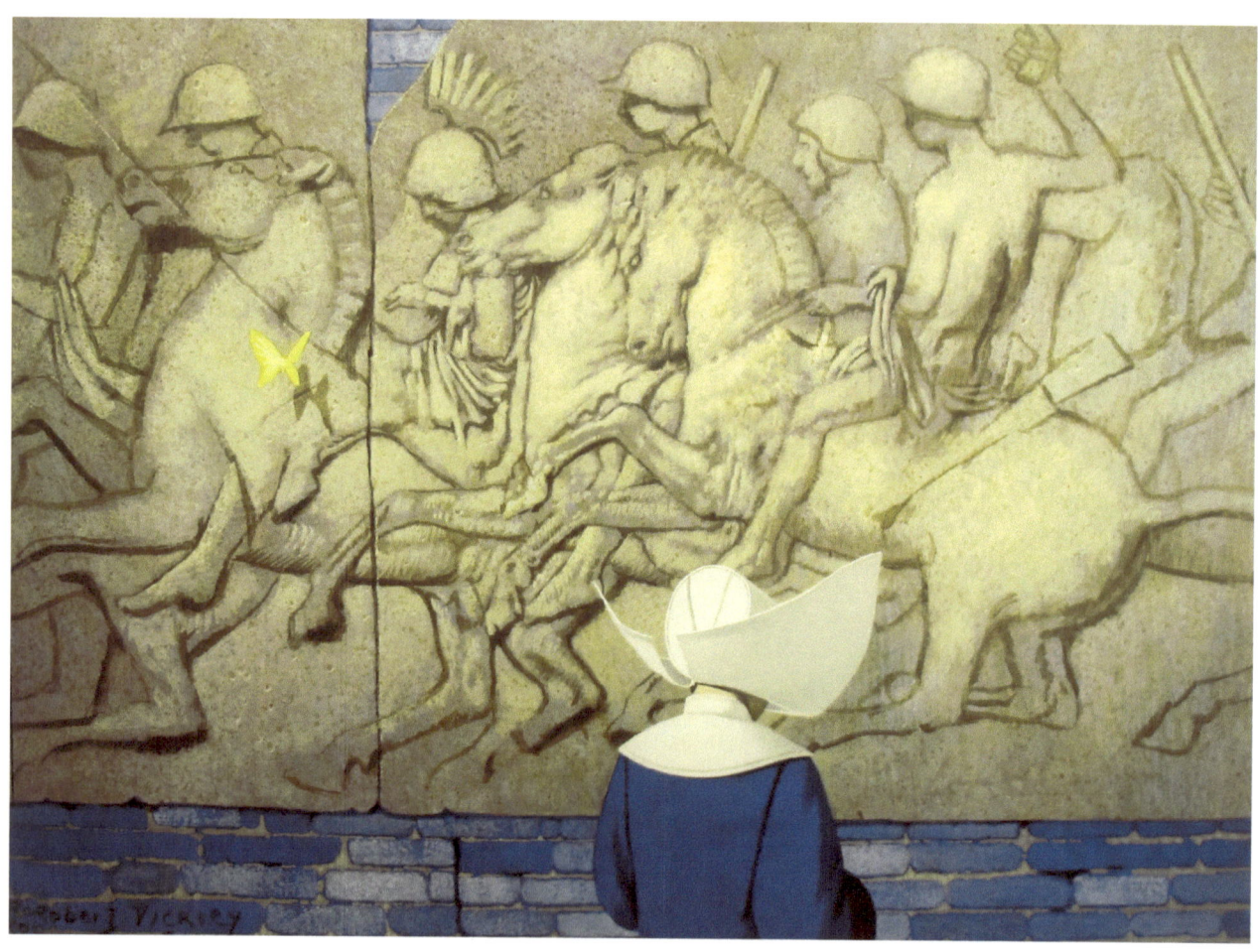

Parthenon Procession, 2002
Egg tempera on gesso on masonite
18 x 24 inches
Harmon-Meek Gallery, Naples

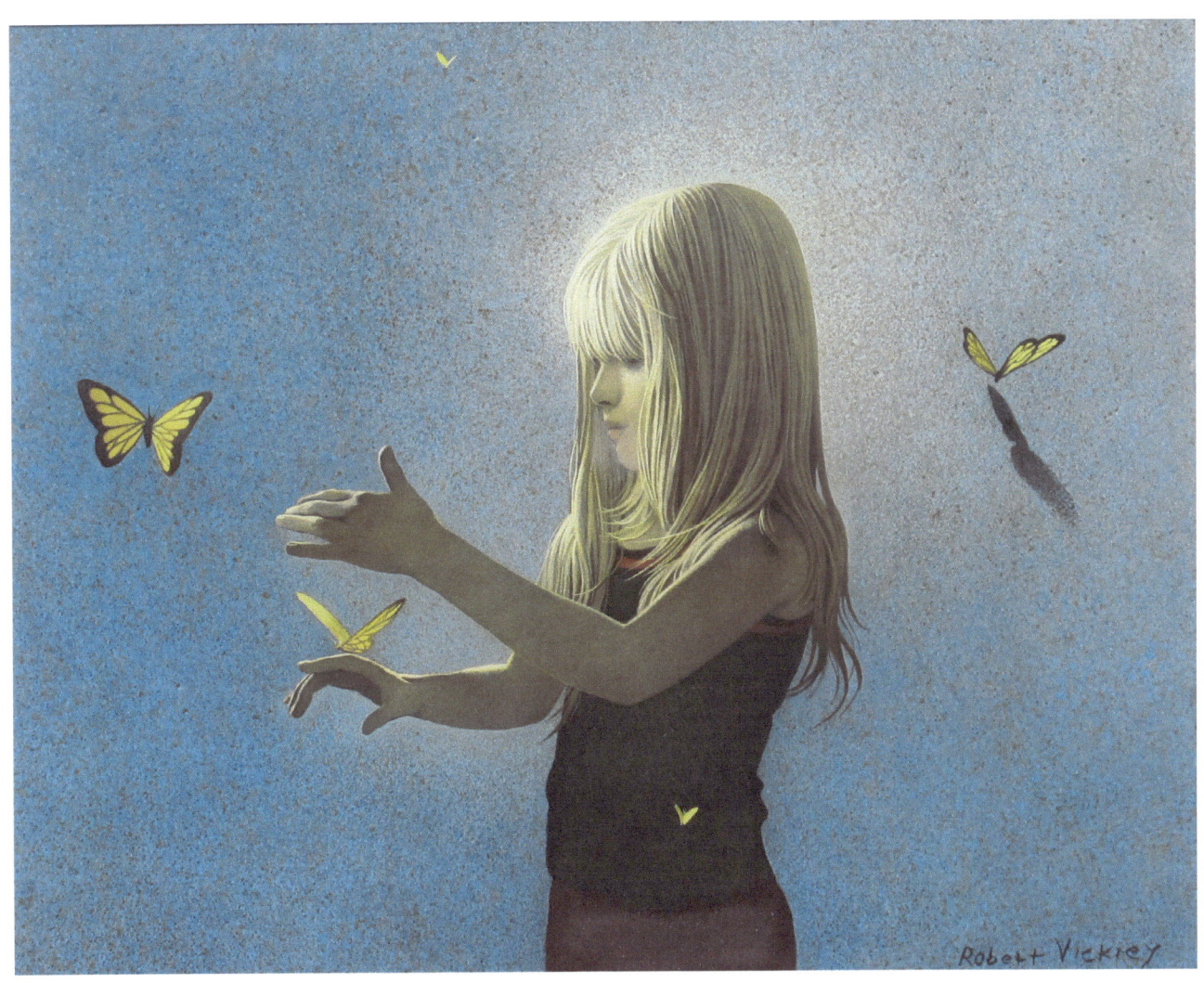

The Chaperone, 2003
Egg tempera on gesso on masonite
16 x 20 inches
William & Barbara Meek

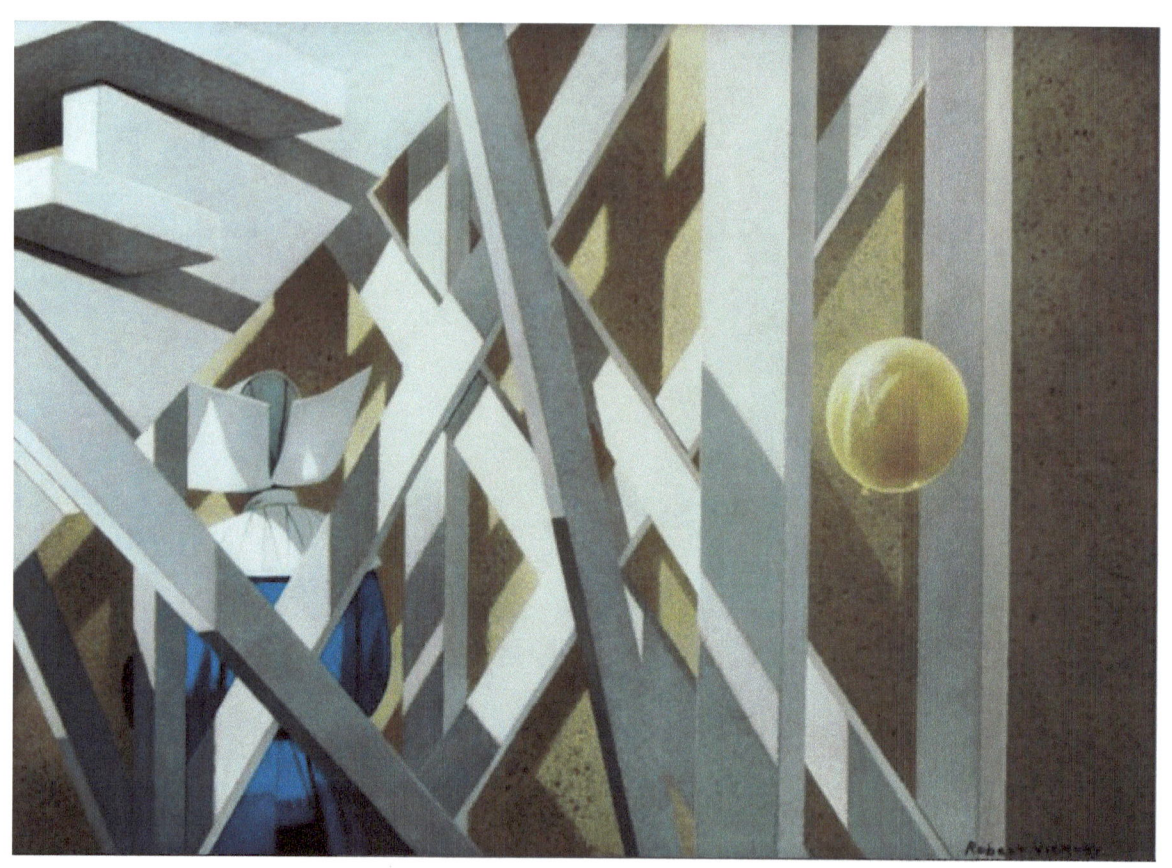

Cathedral of Light, 2003
Egg tempera on gesso on masonite
16 x 22 1/2 inches
Harmon-Meek Gallery, Naples

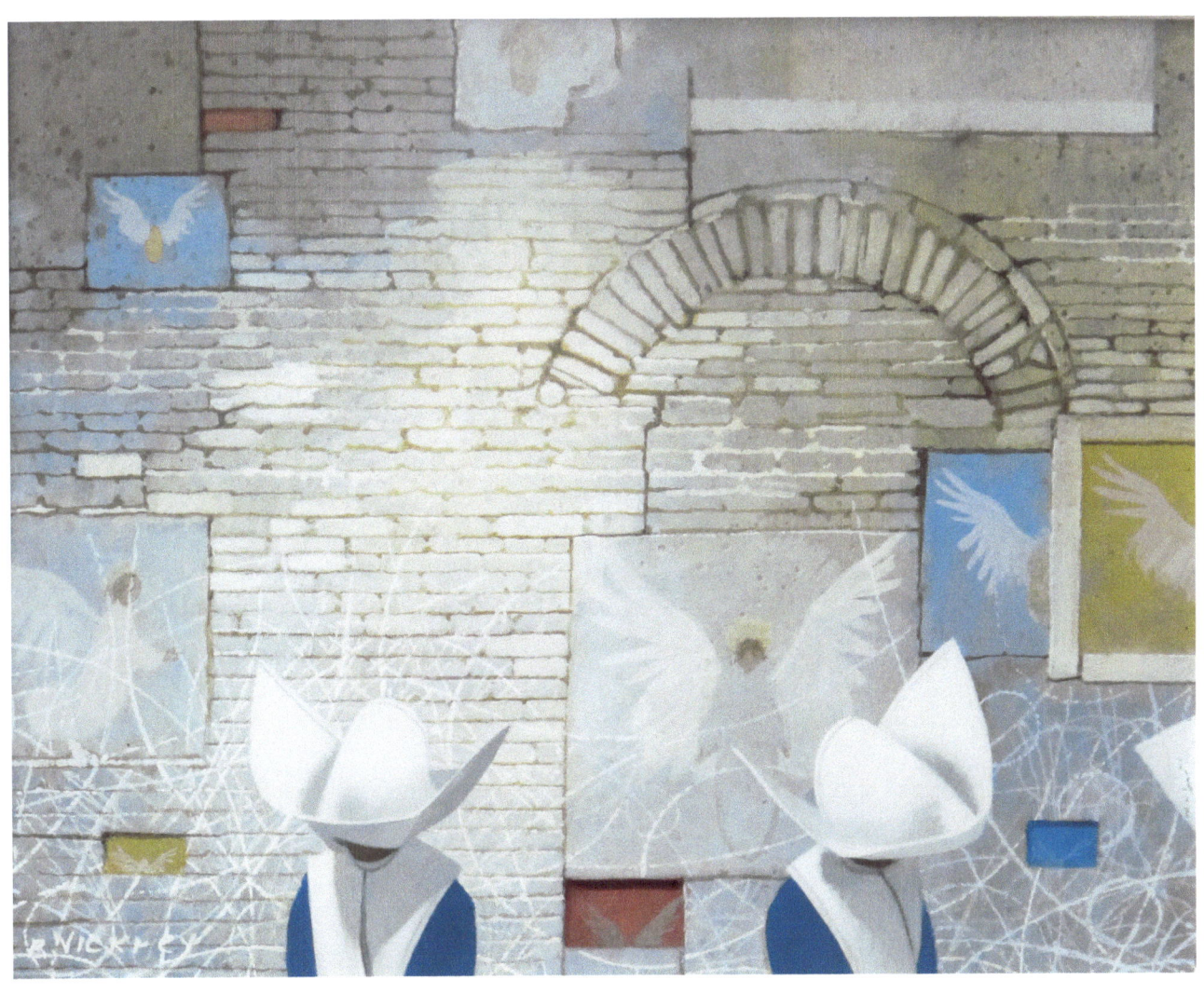

Exaltation of Angels, 2003
Egg tempera on gesso on masonite
8 x 10 inches
Harmon-Meek Gallery, Naples

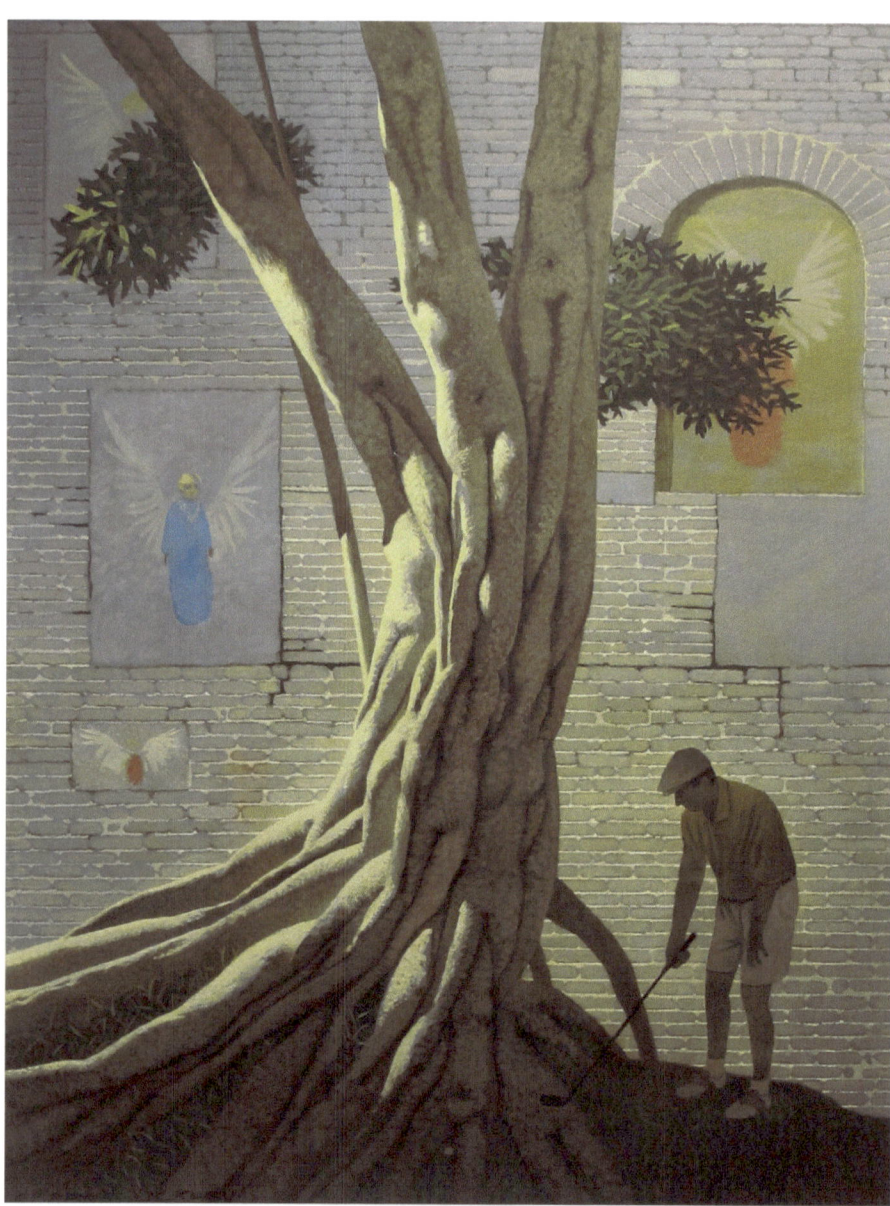

A Difficult Lie, 2006
Egg tempera on gesso on masonite
24 x 18 inches
William & Barbara Meeks

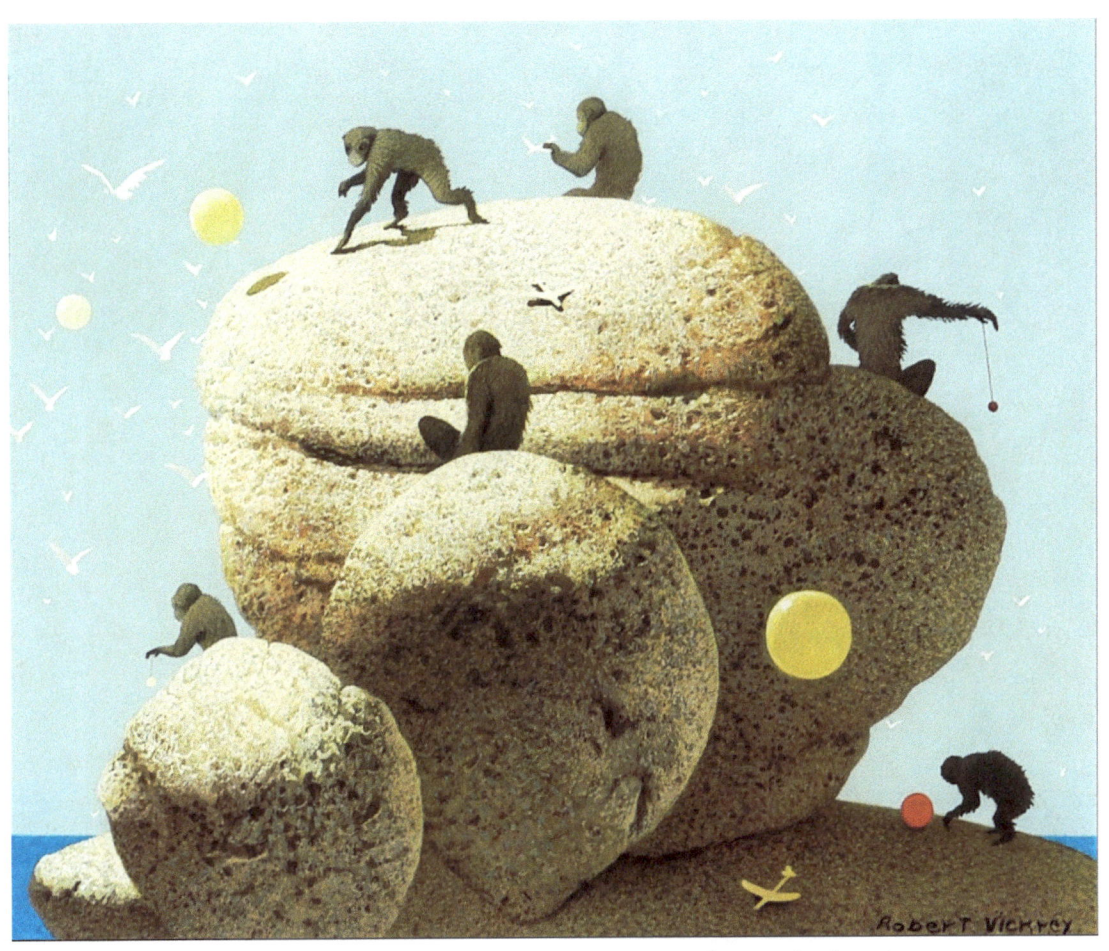

Play Time (Evolution), 2007
Egg tempera on gesso on masonite
12 x 15 inches
Golisano Children's Museum of Naples

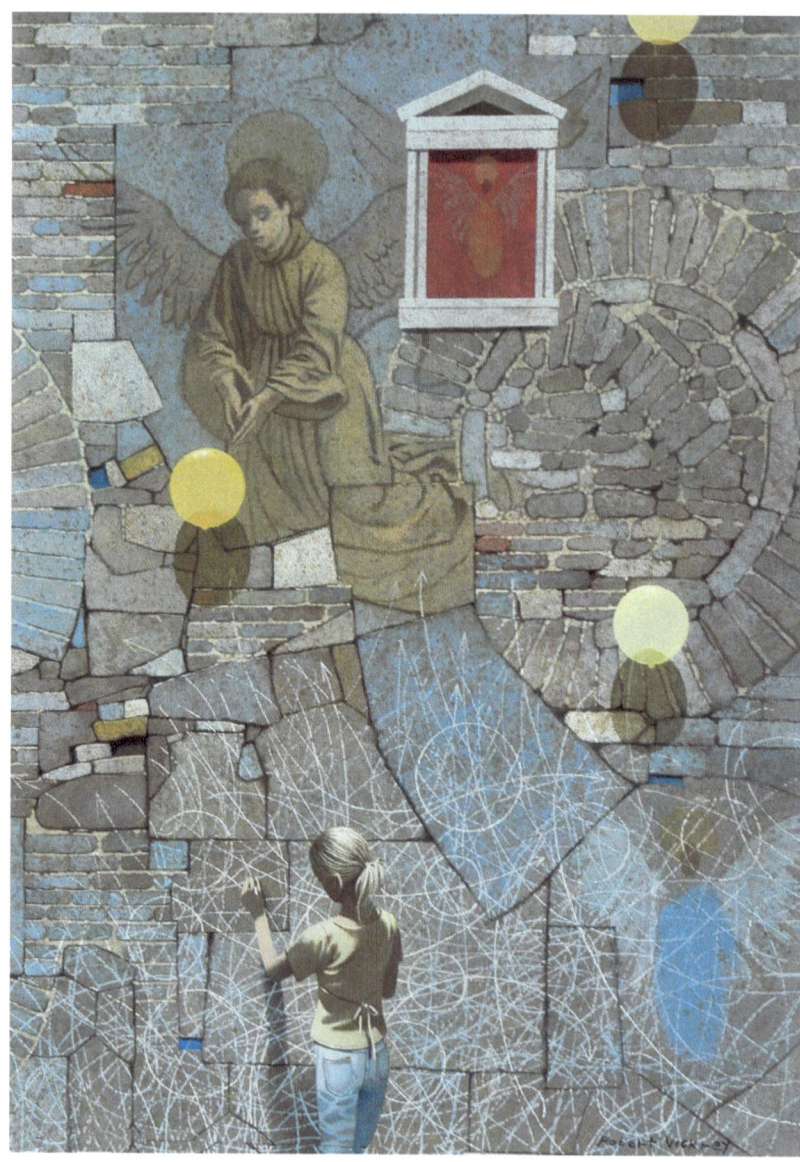

Haloes & Balloons, 2007
Egg tempera on gesso on masonite
32 x 34 inches
Harmon-Meek Gallery, Naples

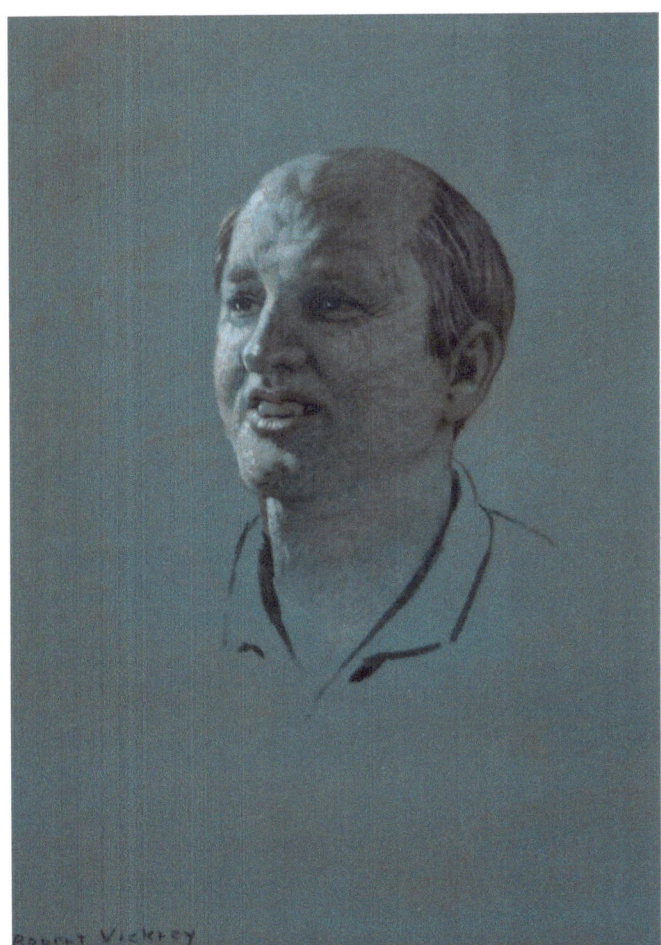

Portrait of WIlliam Meek, 2008
Tempera on paperboard
12 x 9 inches
William & Barbara Meek

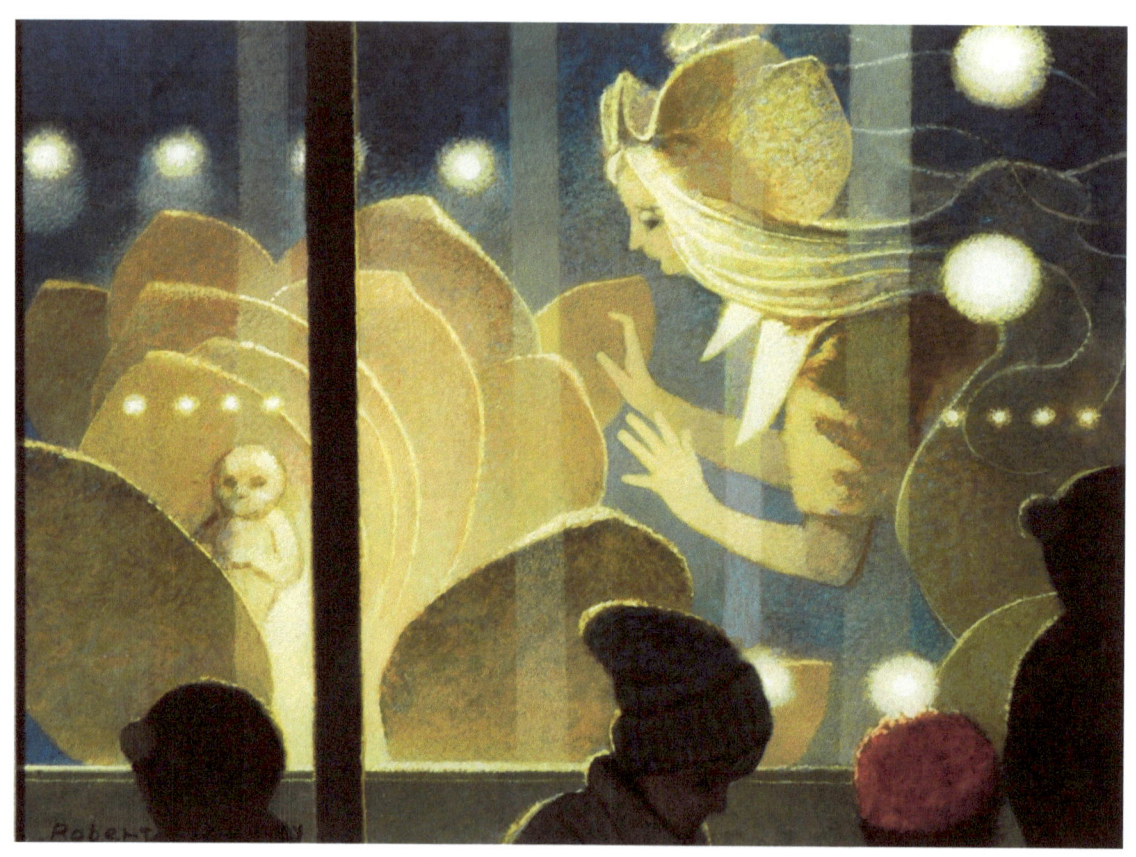

Flower Baby, 2008
Egg tempera on gesso on masonite
12 x 15 inches
Harmon-Meek Gallery, Naples

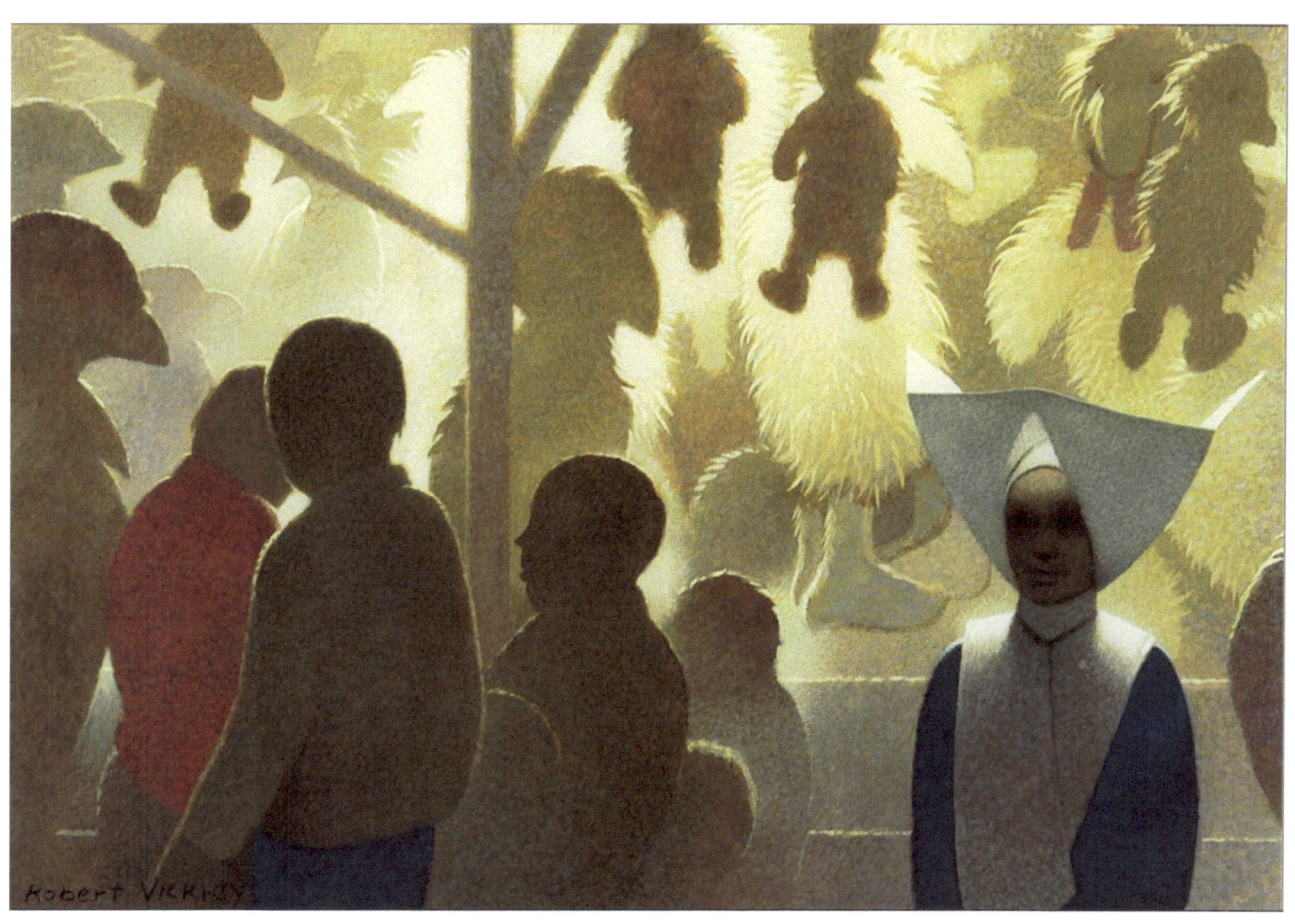

Big Bird Booth, 2008
Egg tempera on gesso on masonite
13 x 19 inches
Harmon-Meek Gallery, Naples

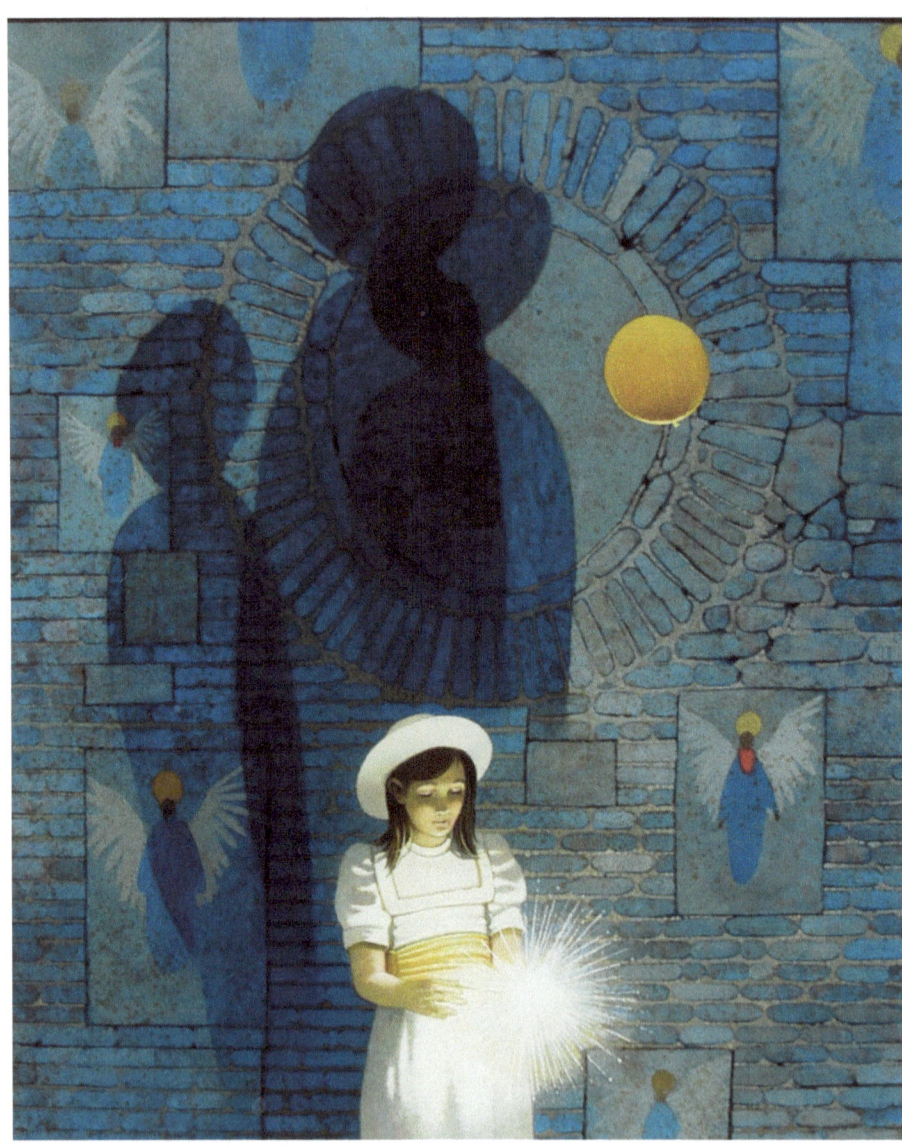

Lacy's Sparkler, 2009
Egg tempera on gesso on masonite
28 3/4 x 22 1/4 inches
Harmon-Meek Gallery, Naples

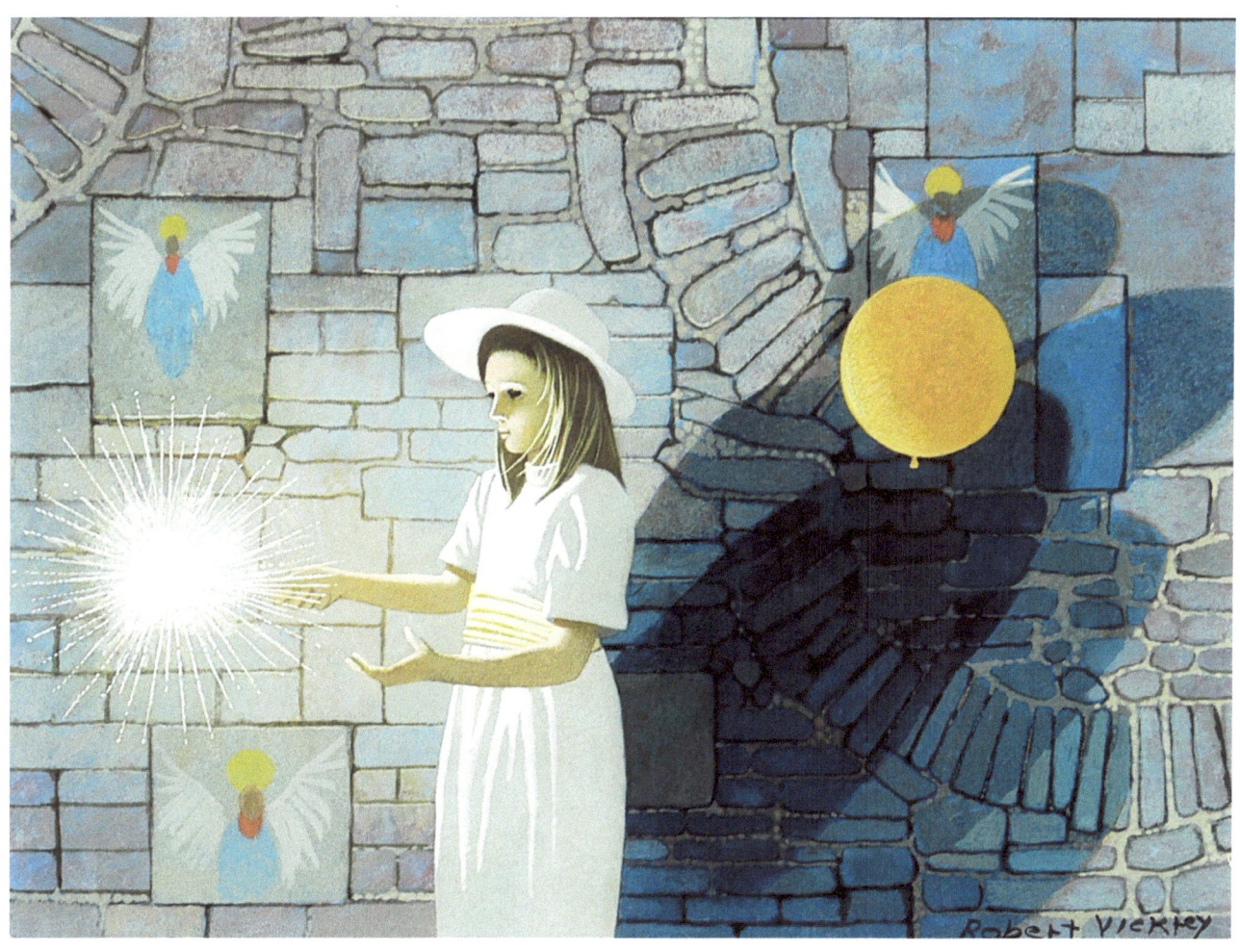

Sparkler Magic, 2009
Egg tempera on gesso on masonite
12 x 16 inches
Harmon-Meek Gallery, Naples

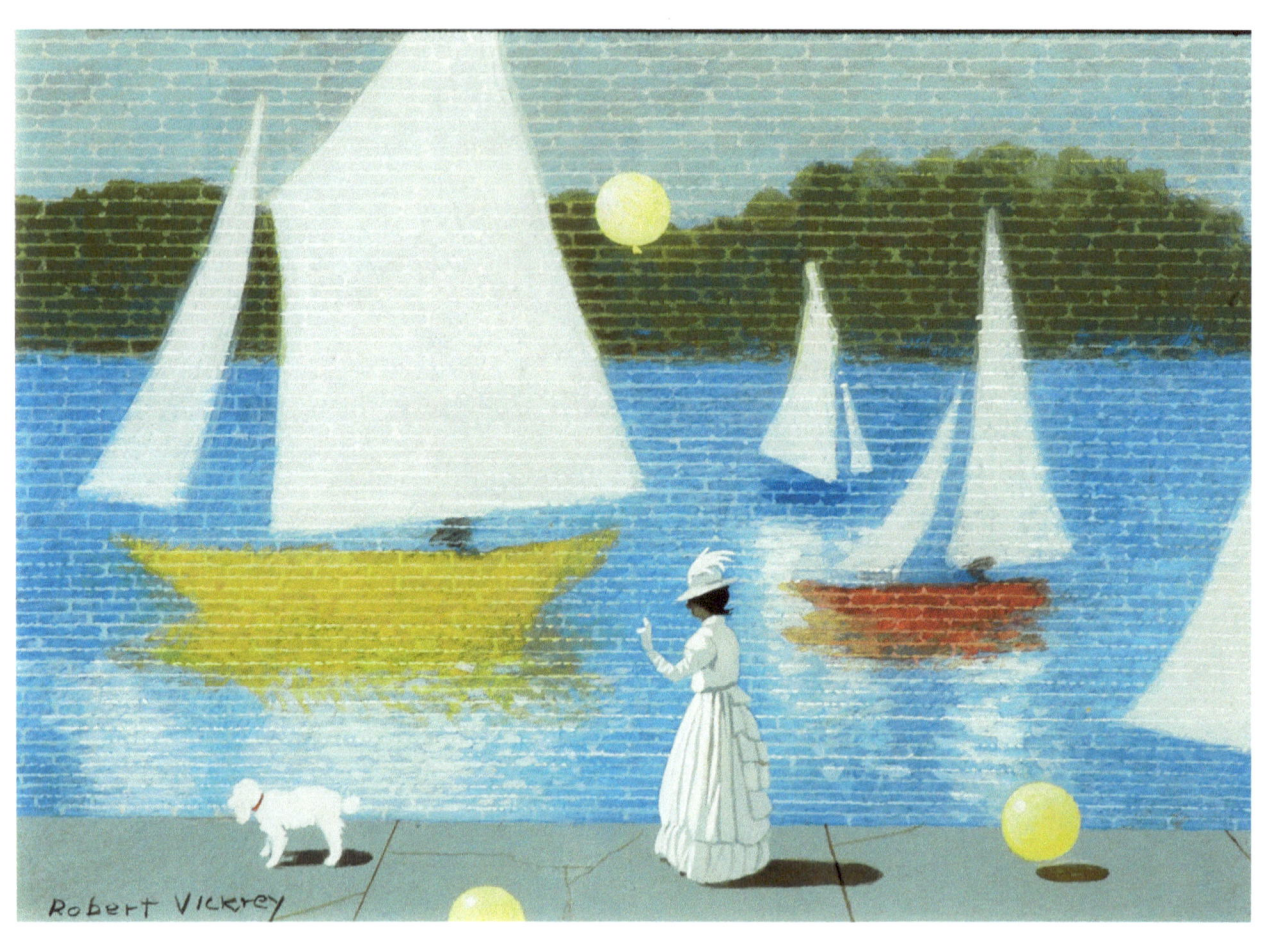

Come Back, Little Sheba, 2009
Egg tempera on gesso on masonite
9 X 12 inches
Harmon-Meek Gallery, Naples

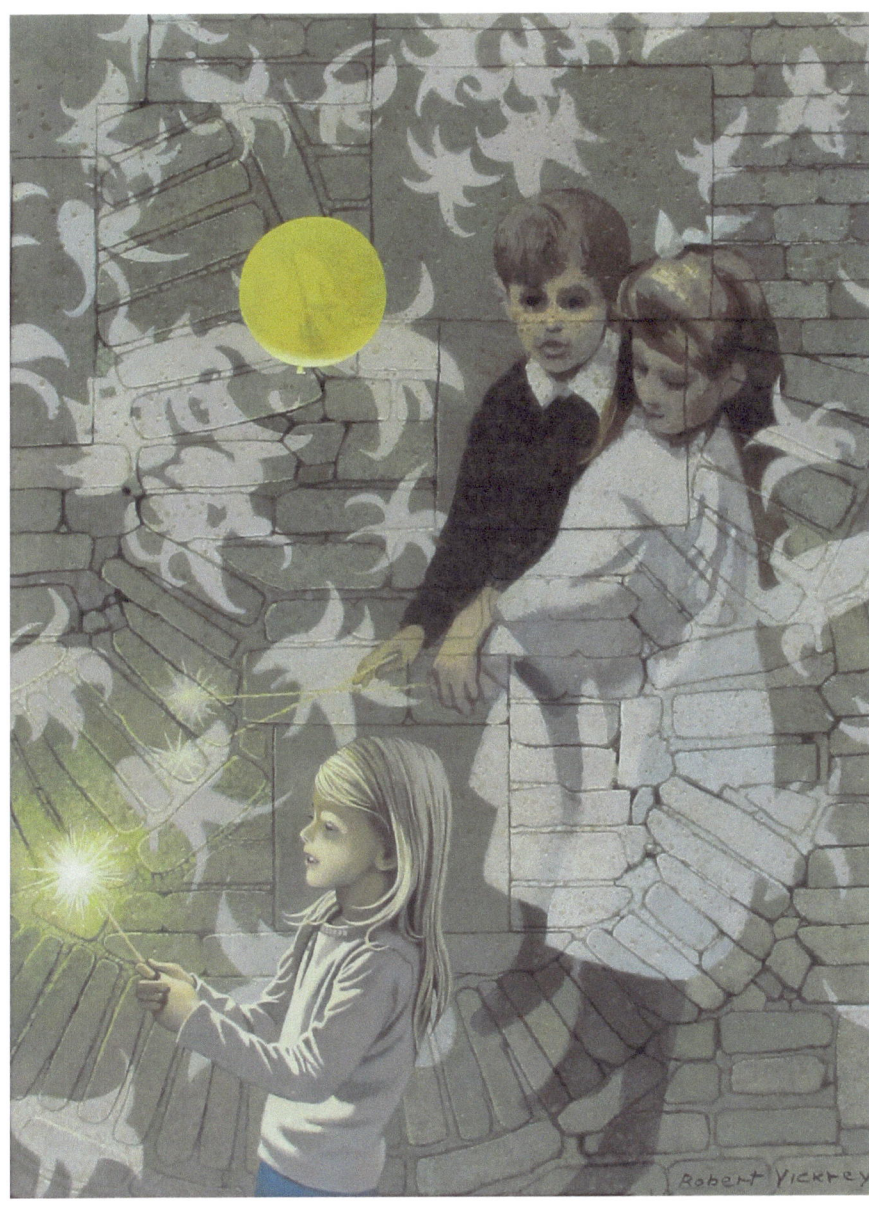

Three Sparklers, 2009
Egg tempera on gesso on masonite
24 1/2 x 18 inches
Harmon-Meek Gallery, Naples

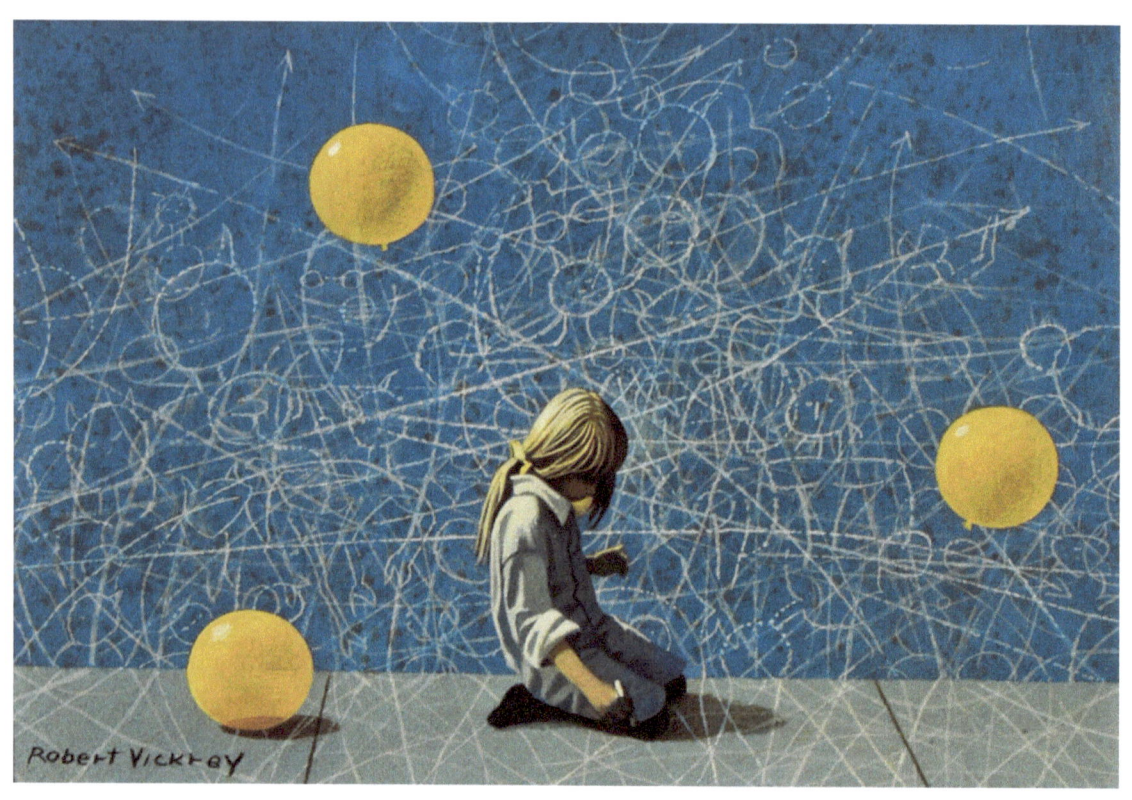

Victoria's Mural, 2010
Egg tempera on gesso on masonite
9 1/4 X 13 1/4 inches
Harmon-Meek Gallery, Naples

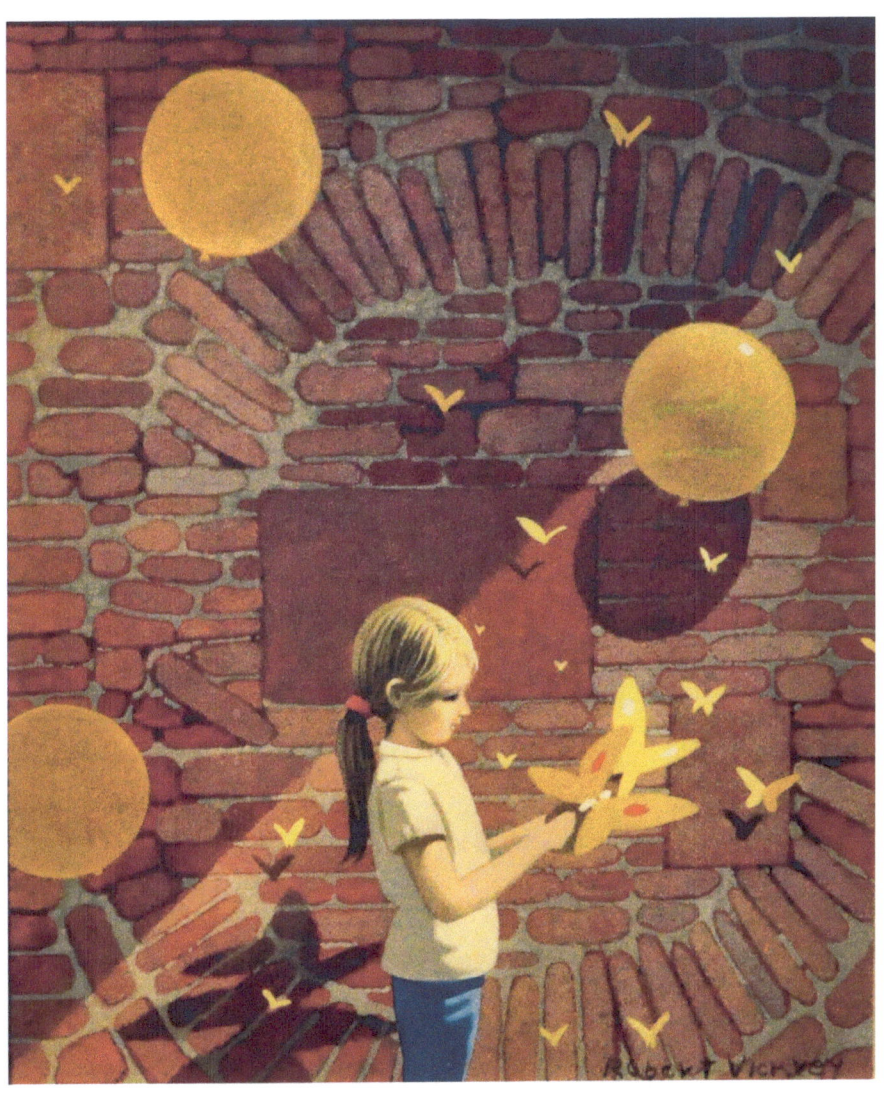

Butterflies Galore, 2010
Egg tempera on gesso on masonite
12 x 10 inches
Harmon-Meek Gallery, Naples

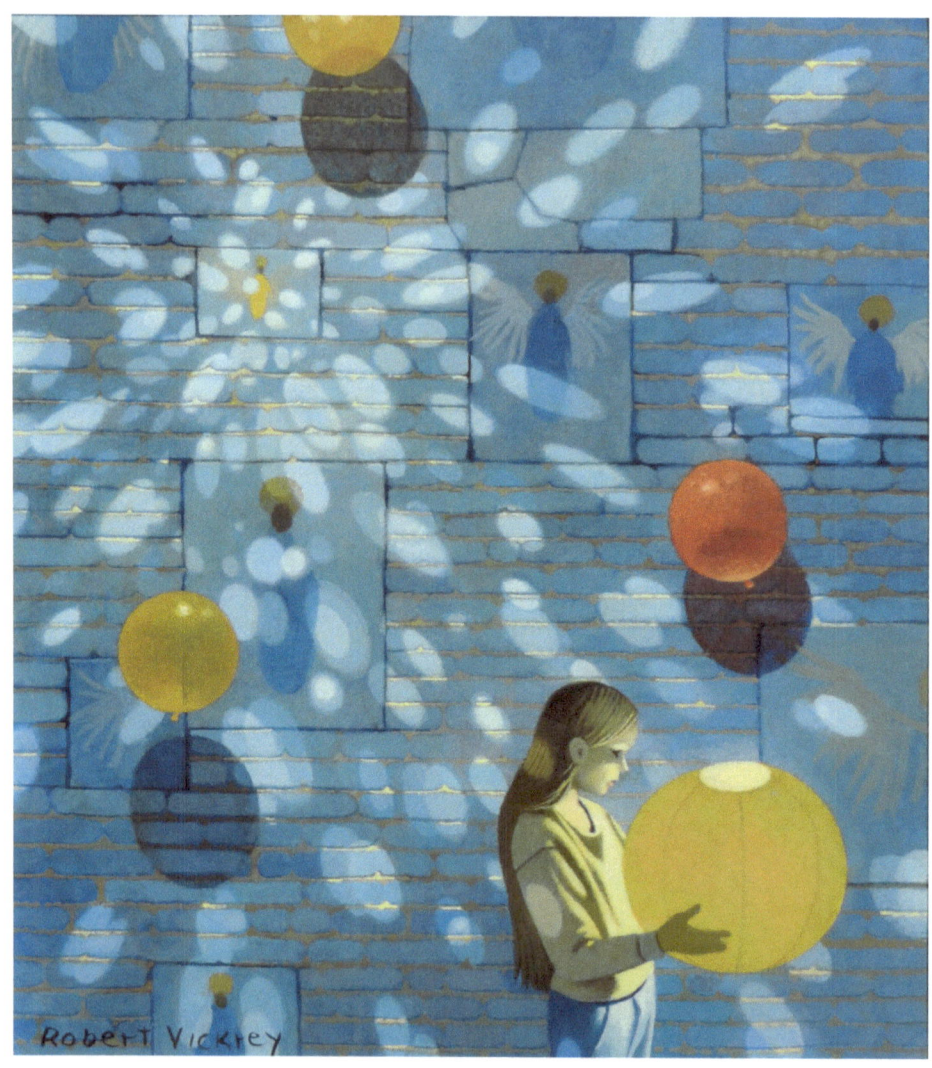

Moonlit Patterns, 2010
Egg tempera on gesso on masonite
14 x 12 inches
Harmon-Meek Gallery, Naples

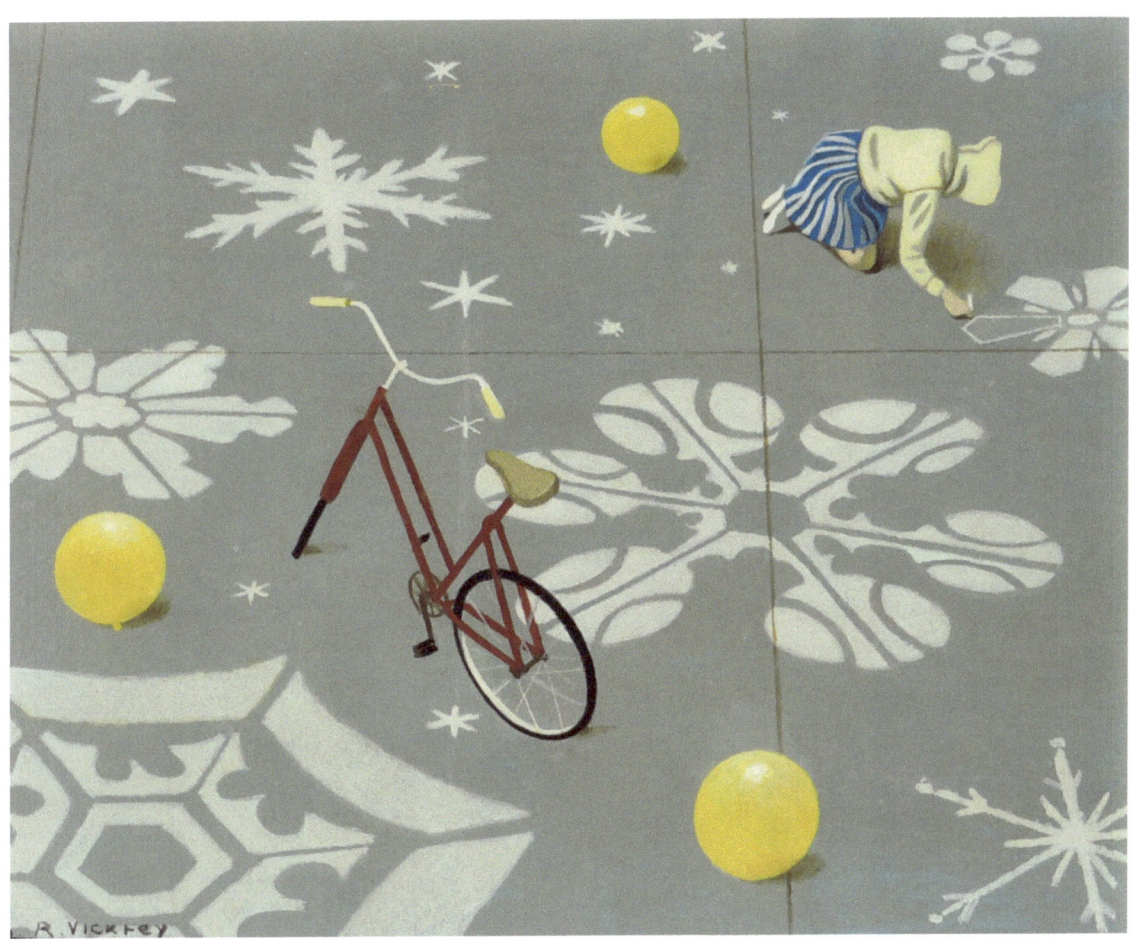

Dreaming of a White Christmas, 2010
Egg tempera on gesso on masonite
8 x 10 inches
Harmon-Meek Gallery, Naples

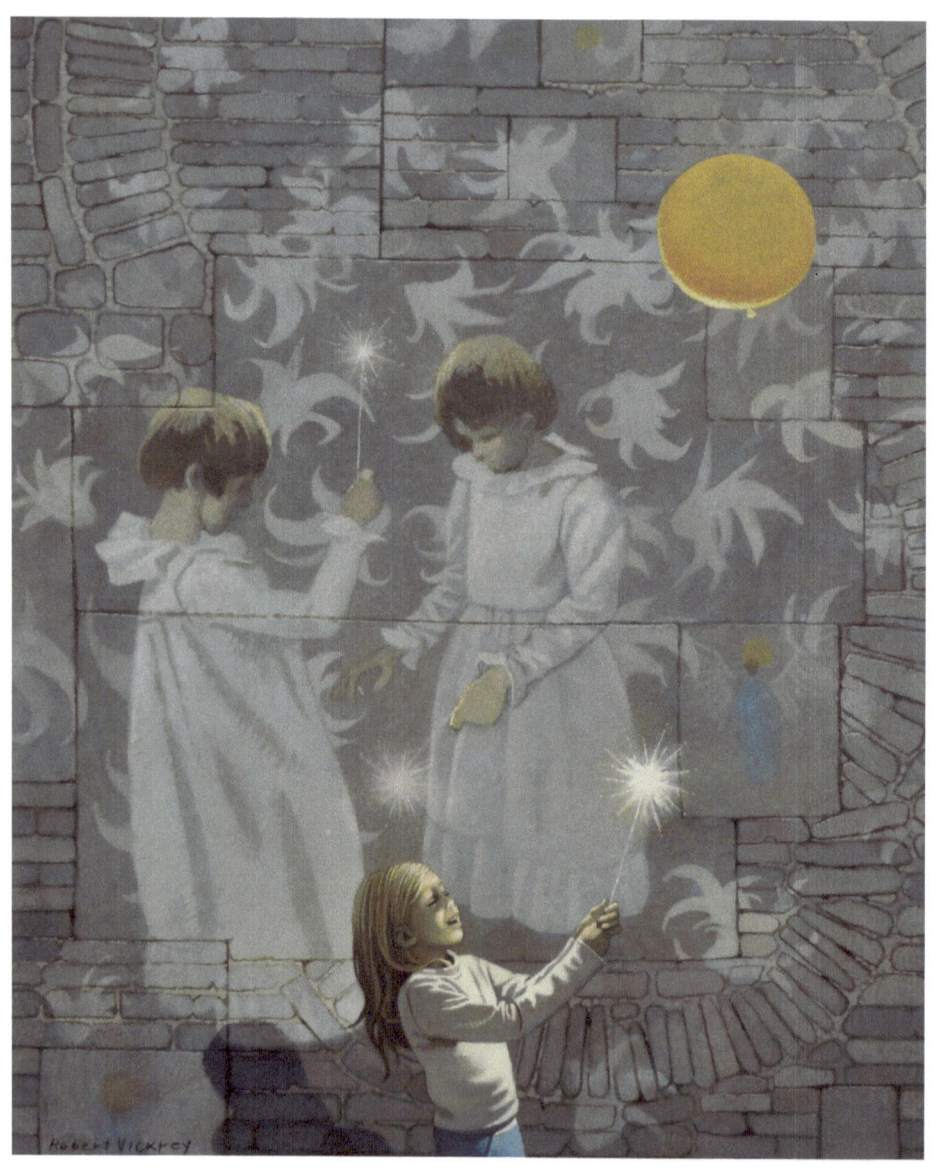

Sargent's Sparklers, 2010
Egg tempera on gesso on masonite
22 1/2 x 17 3/4 inches
Harmon-Meek Gallery, Naples

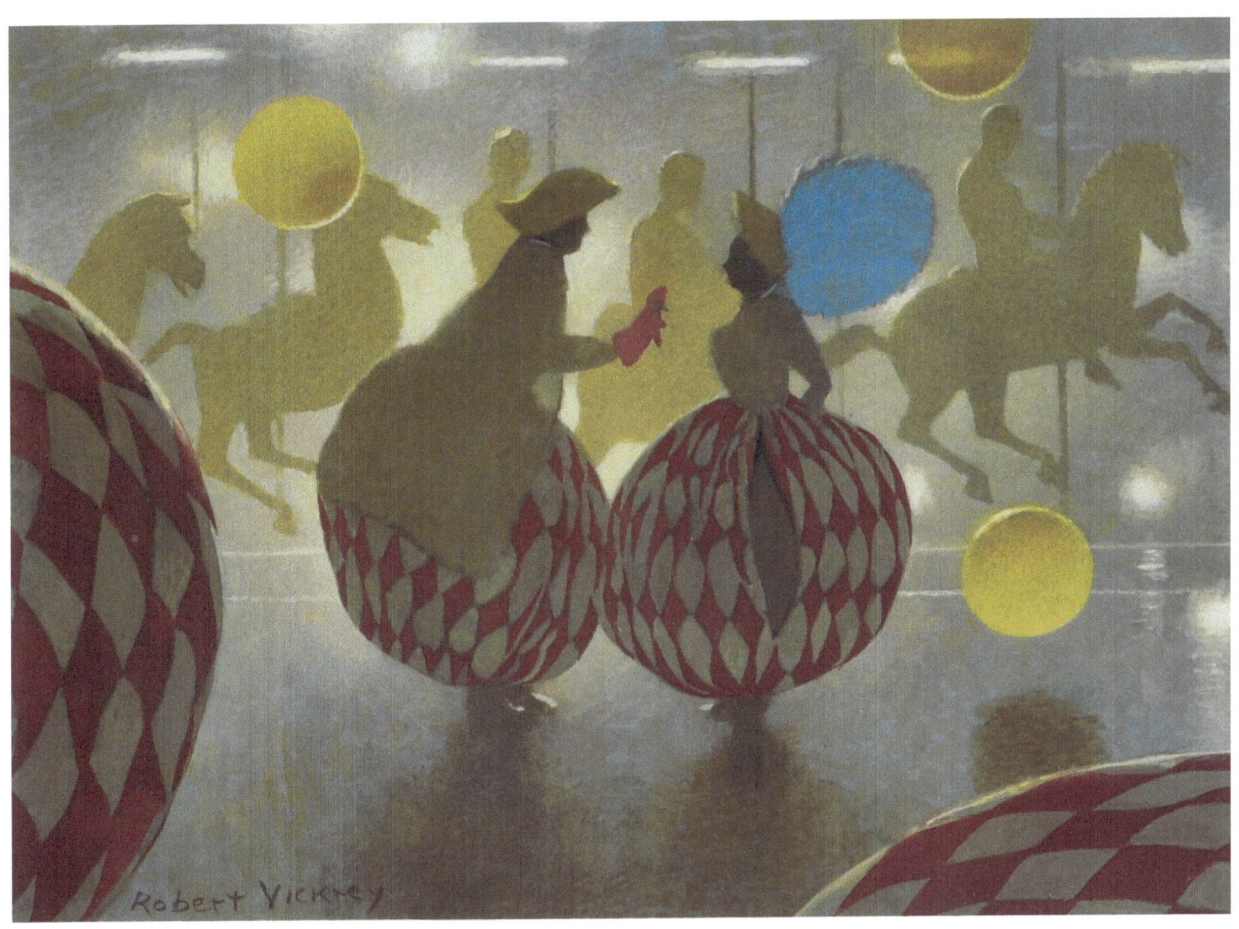

Clowns with Balloon Pants, 2011
Signed (work in progress)
Egg tempera on gesso on masonite
9 x 11 1/2 inches
Harmon-Meek Gallery, Naples

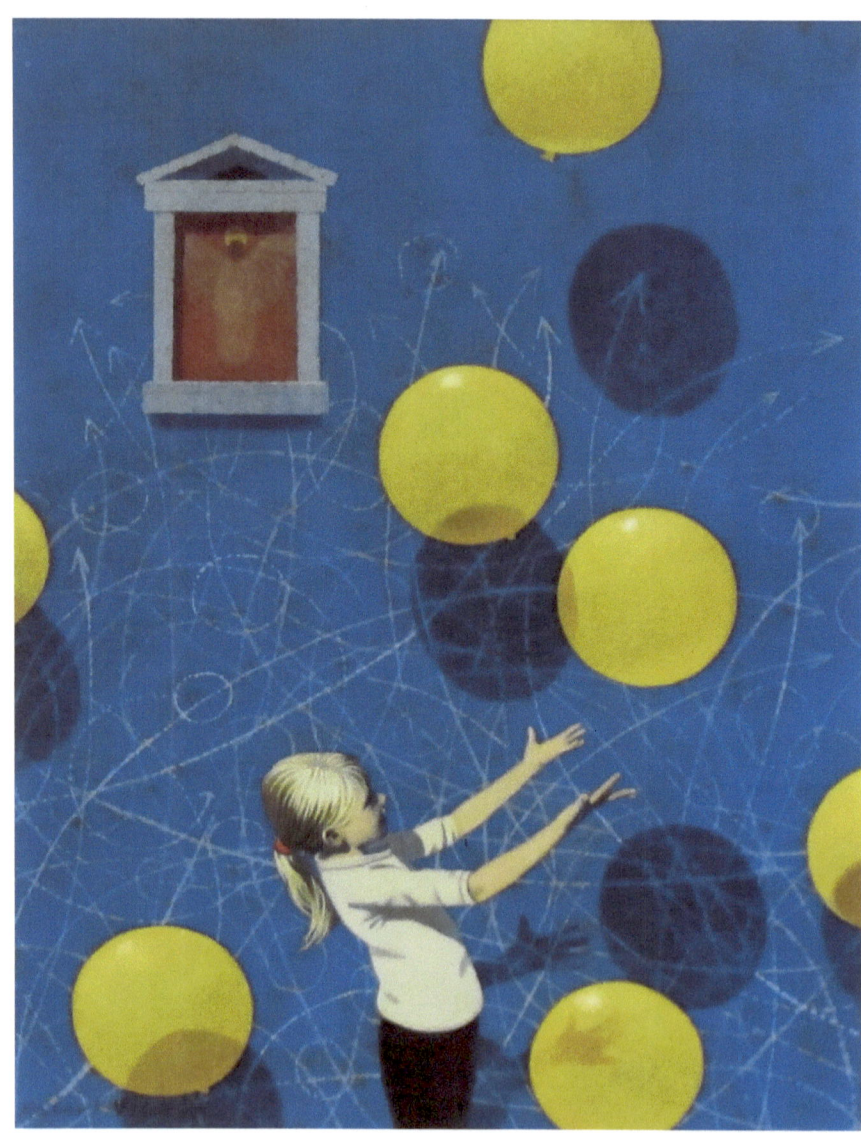

Balloons Balloons, 2011
Egg tempera on gesso on masonite
17 x 13 inches
Harmon-Meek Gallery, Naples

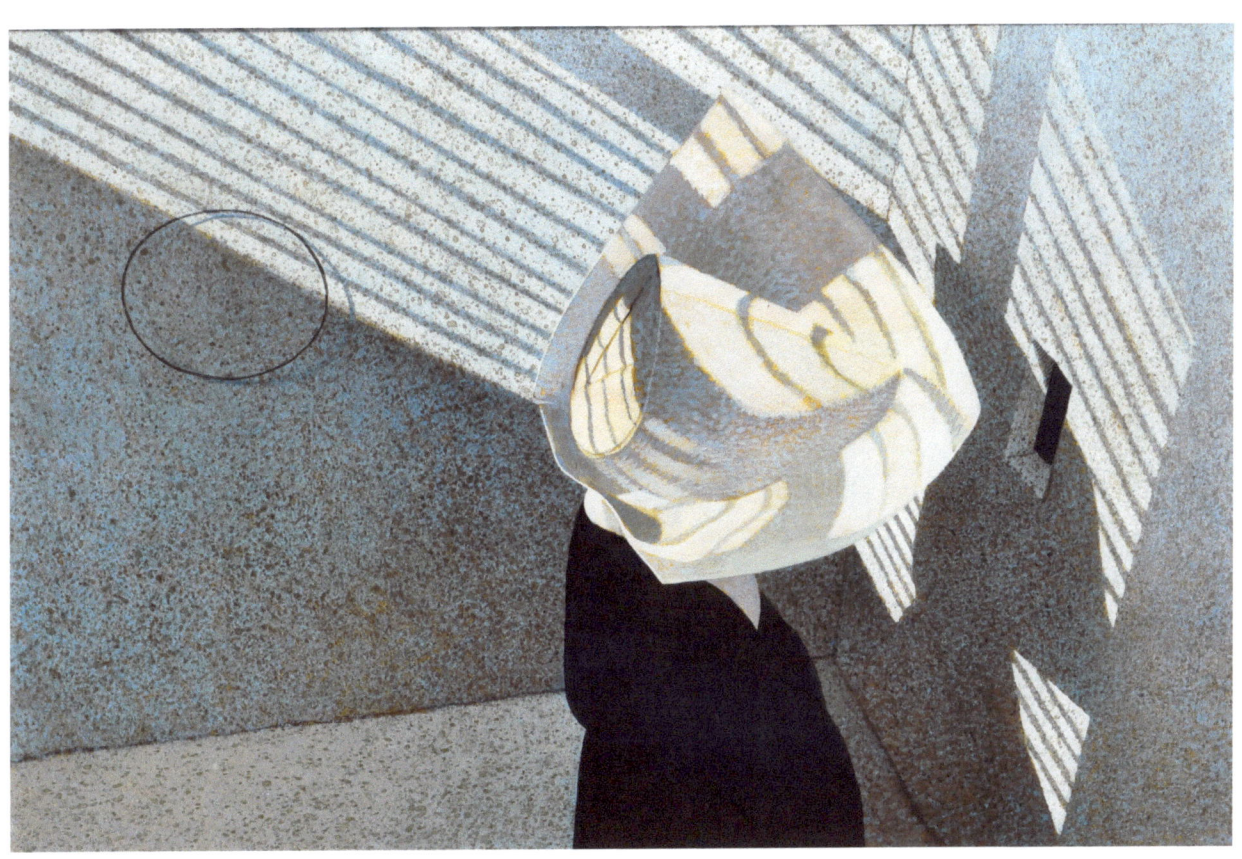

Nun in Corner, 2011
Signed on back (work in progress)
Egg tempera on gesso on masonite
14 x 21 inches
Harmon-Meek Gallery, Naples

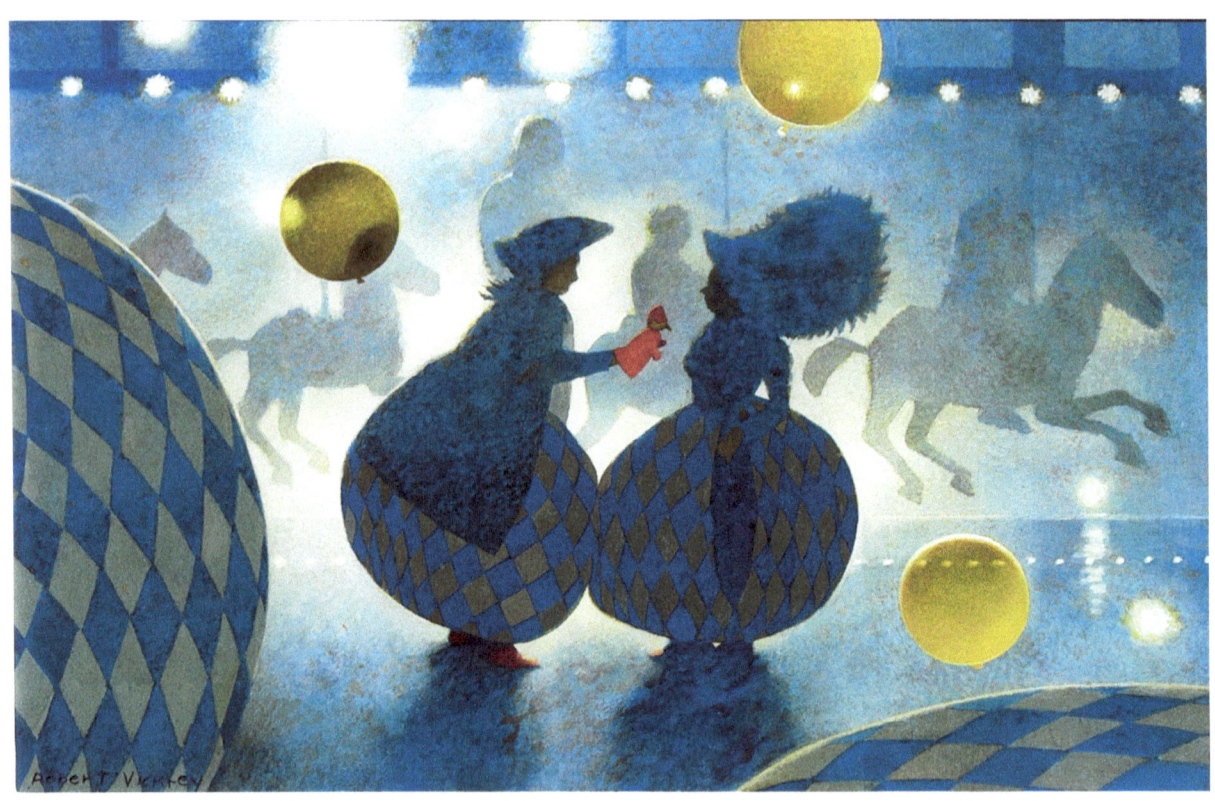

Carnival Night, 2011
Egg tempera on gesso on masonite
16 1/2 x 26 inches
Golisano Children's Museum of Naples

Acknowledgements

The Melvin Gallery and Florida Southern College would like to thank the following individuals and institutions for their generosity and contributions to this important and exciting exhibition.

Most special thanks go to William Meek (FSC '72), director emeritus of the Harmon-Meek Gallery in Naples, Florida, who curated this exhibition exclusively for our galleries, lending pieces from the personal collection of Vickrey's works he and his wife Barbara Hanson Meek (FSC '76) have amassed over the decades and from those available for sale at the family gallery, as well as securing loans from other collectors and area institutions to create a more comprehensive retrospective. The amount of time, effort, and attention to detail Mr. Meek offered — in all aspects of putting this exhibition together — far exceeds a typical alumnus' love for his alma mater. We are most grateful.

We also thank Juliana Meek, the director-owner of the Harmon-Meek Gallery, for her help and willingness to lend from her personal collection as well for our show.

Thank you also to Carrie Cutchens, Curator of Collections at the Golisano Children's Museum of Naples, for her part in lending two works from C'MON for this exhibition.

Very special thanks also to James Rogers, director emeritus of the Melvin Gallery, for his essential role in requesting the exhibition from Mr. Meek and to Ann Gurley Rogers and Jim, both, for their assistance reading over this catalogue and for offering their sage exhibition-planning advice.

Finally, thank you to Jenna Rice, our outgoing departmental assistant and devoted curator of the Melvin Gallery, whose dedication to the Department and to the hangings and preparations of our shows over the past two academic years has made her not only a hard act for our next assistant/curator, Diane Baires, to follow but has also made her a part of our Art Department family forever.

— *H. Alexander Rich*

www.ingramcontent.com/pod-product-compliance
Lightning Source LLC
Chambersburg PA
CBHW051025180526
45172CB00002B/469